A Little Night Music

Model for one of Michael Anania's sets for the New York City Opera production

A Little Night Music

●

Music and Lyrics by
Stephen Sondheim

Book by
Hugh Wheeler

Suggested by a Film by Ingmar Bergman

Originally Produced and Directed on Broadway by Harold Prince

Introduction by Jonathan Tunick

APPLAUSE THEATRE BOOK PUBLISHERS
211 West 71 St. New York, N.Y. 10023

All inquiries concerning stock, amateur, second-class touring and foreign language stage performing rights should be directed to Music Theatre International, 545 Eighth Avenue, New York, N.Y. 10018.

Inquiries concerning all other rights should be addressed to Flora Roberts, c/o Flora Roberts, Inc., 157 West 57th Street, New York, N.Y. 10019 and William Morris Agency, Inc., 1350 Avenue of the Americas, New York, N.Y. 10019, Attn: Samuel Liff.

Grateful acknowledgement is made to the following for permission to include their photographs and scene and costume designs: Van Williams, Zoë Dominic, Concorde-New Horizons Corp./Wein Film Gmbh/Polygram Pictures, Martha Swope Associates/Carol Rosegg, Boris Aronson, Florence Klotz, Michael Anania and Lindsay W. Davis.

Drawing by Hirschfeld Copyright © 1973 by Al Hirschfeld and reproduced by special arrangement with Hirschfeld's exclusive representative, The Margo Feiden Galleries Ltd., New York.

Design by Gary Denys.

Library of Congress Cataloging-in-Publication Data
Sondheim, Stephen.
    [Little night music. Libretto]
    A little night music / book by Hugh Wheeler; music and lyrics by Stephen Sondheim ; based on a film by Ingmar Bergman ; introduction by Jonathan Tunick.
       p. cm. – (Applause musical library)
    Libretto of a musical.
    Discography: p.
    ISBN 1-55783-069-X : $19.95. – ISBN 1-55783-070-3 (pbk.) : $9.95
    1. Musicals–Librettos. I. Wheeler, Hugh. II. Bergman, Ingmar, 1918-   . III. Title.
IV. Series.
    ML50.S705L6 1990 <Case>   90-40230
    782.1'4'-268–dc20   CIP
                                                        MN

Manufactured in the United States of America

APPLAUSE THEATRE BOOK PUBLISHERS
211 West 71st Street
New York, New York 10023

First Applause Printing, 1991

CONTENTS

INTRODUCTION

During the course of our preliminary discussions of *A Little Night Music,* Stephen Sondheim remarked that he imagined "the atmosphere to be perfumed—of musk in the air." My immediate reply was, "Plenty of strings." This exchange offers a paradigm of the composer-orchestrator relationship as practiced in the Broadway musical. Although the various textbook definitions of the orchestrator's craft confine themselves strictly to the adaptation for orchestra of music already complete in melody, harmony, and form, but composed for another medium, such as the piano, the theater orchestrator's responsibilities are more far-reaching. It is his function, as indicated by the foregoing anecdote, to translate into practical terms the musical and dramatic conception of the composer, who, unlike Sondheim, may not be a literate, trained musician, or, like him, may conceive his music exclusively on the piano and need to rely upon a specialist in the technique of the orchestra and its various instruments. Sondheim is rare among Broadway composers in that he calls for highly colored and dramatic effects in his accompaniments, but typical in that he is not trained in translating these effects from the medium of the piano to that of the orchestra.

Therefore, the existence of what I have come to regard as an honorable craft and the opportunity for me to have participated in the creation of this most elegant work.

If one imagines the Sondheim-Prince musicals of the 1970s to be the movements of a symphony (*Company:*

1

Allegro; *Follies:* Adagio; *Pacific Overtures*—well I admit that the analogy falters here—how about Intermezzo á l'Orientale; and *Sweeney Todd:* Finale), *A Little Night Music* takes its place as the third, or Scherzo, movement. The Scherzo, introduced by Beethoven as a replacement for the Classical symphony's Minuet, became an integral element of the Romantic symphonies of Schubert, Mendelssohn, and Brahms.

A Little Night Music, like the Scherzo, is light, fast, playful, mysterious, and in triple meter. It swims in the heady, magical atmosphere imagined by its creators and displays all the literacy and wit that we have come to expect from them. The music is rich in melodic invention, contrapuntal development, and harmonic texture. The show's quirky, appealing characters demonstrate satisfying growth during the course of the developing plot, which comes to a rational and gratifying conclusion. It is Prince's most romantic work as well: erotic, charming, and imaginative.

Although easier on the audience than most of Sondheim's musicals, *A Little Night Music* is by no means simplistic. Like all great romantic works, it is classically precise in structure. Hugh Wheeler brought to the material the exactitude of the mystery writer (Sondheim commented that the show is plotted like an Iris Murdoch novel), creating between the various characters an effectively geometrical pattern of interrelationships, based, like the score, upon the number three:

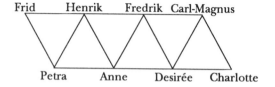

A chain of triangles: in each of these connected relationships, the unstable number three is drawn to the stable two, as the various mismatched couples disengage and find their proper partners.

It was Sondheim's intention that the score be entirely in triple time—a Waltz musical in the style of the turn-of-the-century Viennese operettas. (Strauss, Lehar, and Kálmán, the masters of this genre, never did this—the many waltzes in their scores are balanced by plenty of music in 2/4 and 4/4—polkas, marches, galops, etc.) Though one might quibble about Sondheim's use of a 12/8 Nocturne pattern accompanying "Send in the Clowns," and that there are twelve 2/4 bars in "The Glamorous Life," eighteen more in "The Miller's Son," and an entire passage in 4/4 (No. 22 in the Vocal Score—an underscoring passage), the remainder of the score consists exclusively of various permutations of triple time, utilizing for the main part eighteenth- and nineteenth-century generic forms such as the Waltz ("Soon," "You Must Meet My Wife"), Mazurka ("Remember," "The Glamorous Life"), Sarabande ("Later," "Liaisons"), Polonaise ("In Praise of Women"), Etude ("Now," "Every Day a Little Death"), and Gigue ("A Weekend in the Country").

There is great symmetry of form here as well as in the book. Sondheim tends here toward trios with the characters separated ("Now," "Later," "Soon") and duets regarding a third person ("You Must Meet My Wife," "It Would Have Been Wonderful," "Every Day a Little Death"). These songs of alienation and yearning for cohesion and balance all represent the unstable number three drawn to the stable two—the triangle yearning to be reconciled to the proper couple. This precision of form is combined with a musky romanticism and all-round good humor and warmth. Here is Sondheim at his very best: witty, whimsical, and knowing.

Sondheim's musicals present an unusual challenge to the orchestrator in that he eschews for the most part the familiar melodic, harmonic, and rhythmic conventions of the Broadway musical. *A Little Night Music* is no exception to this principle, presenting as it does some particularly harrowing problems, such as the cross-hand Etude pattern in the accompaniment of "Every Day a Little Death." The syncopated eighth-note pattern was originally assigned to the clarinets, who quickly retitled the piece "Every Page a Little Breath" due to the complete absence of rests in their part. (The company was unusually partial to puns and parodies—I recall with particular pleasure Barbara Lang's "The screens won't move, they keep falling out of their groove" to the tune of "Night Waltz.") For the movie version, I thought better of the situation and scored the passage for the nonbreathing strings.

Sondheim provided his typically complete piano accompaniment for each song, meticulously notated as to melody, harmony, and rhythm—much like an art-song accompaniment—and most effective when performed in its original medium—the piano. Although I have never heard him play a note written by another composer (with the single exception of "Something's Coming" from *West Side Story*, accompanying Larry Kert at a party), Sondheim plays his own compositions most effectively on the piano and sings the parts of the various characters, usually, like Leonard Bernstein, at an octave below pitch. His piano accompaniments, like those of art songs, suggest the dramatic implications of the songs and their appropriate instrumentation through use of rhythmic, contrapuntal, and coloristic devices such as repeated notes, arpeggios, broken chords, and the use of extreme registers.

Because these devices are idiomatic only to the piano, and are ineffective or even impossible to play on orchestral instruments, the accompaniments must be reduced by the orchestrator to a harmonic and rhythmic abstraction and recomposed, utilizing devices suitable to orchestral combinations. This process results in a full orchestral score that bears little visual resemblance to the original piano accompaniment, and when the orchestral score is reduced by the copyist to a short score or piano-conductor part, thereby reversing the orchestration process, the written notes, now reflecting orchestral rather than piano idioms, suffer in effect when played on the piano.

Aside from developing a general familiarity with the score by having it played and sung by the composer in person and on tape recordings and reading it at home, as well as some general research into the musical and historical milieu of the place (in this case the waltzes of Strauss and Lehar, and late Romantic music in general, particularly Russian and Scandinavian—Tchaikovsky, Rachmaninoff, and Grieg), there is little for the orchestrator to do until the rehearsal period begins. Not until then is it decided what keys will be appropriate for the various performers—they are invariably different from those in which the songs are originally written—and the songs are expanded by the director and choreographer, working with the dance music arranger at the piano, into full-length numbers. I have wasted what seem to be cubic miles of breath trying to explain to inexperienced producers that any orchestration done before the rehearsal period will invariably be thrown out. The production must be orchestrated as much as the score, and the rehearsal period is as much a creative process as the writing; it cannot be second-guessed.

During the time before the rehearsal period, the orchestrator may plan his instrumentation. The size of a Broadway orchestra is determined by an agreement between the League of New York Theaters and Local 802 of the American Federation of Musicians, specifying a minimum number of players for each theater. Although it is not unheard of, it is rare indeed for a producer to agree to engage more than the minimum number of players. The minimum, therefore, becomes effectively the maximum.

At the time of *A Little Night Music* the minimum at the Shubert Theater was twenty-five players, a typical number for a Broadway musical. With such a limited number of musicians available, every player counts, and the orchestrator must choose his instrumentation with great care and accuracy, giving particular attention to balance between sections. (To balance seven brass and five saxophones, for example, against six violins and two 'cellos is quite a feat, although it can be and has been done.)

Since *A Little Night Music* is European in setting, turn-of-the-century in time, and romantic in style, and since the score reflects these qualities, containing no musical anachronisms or stylistic deviations, I decided upon a legitimate operetta orchestra, not dependent upon a rhythm section but fully orchestrated in Classical style, and employing traditional combinations of woodwind, brass, string, and percussion instruments, foregoing such inappropriate ones as saxophones and guitars. The score is so delicate that I was tempted to dispense with the trumpets and drums, but decided to include them for safety's sake. It was, after all, a Broadway musical, a field in which no one has ever suffered due to lack of subtlety.

The instrumentation that I planned was that of a typical operetta orchestra, but held to a somewhat inadequate number of strings mandated by Broadway budgets. It is composed of the following:

Five woodwinds: flute, oboe, two clarinets, and bassoon, each player alternating on one or more doubles, or secondary instruments, such as the piccolo, English horn, bass clarinet, and so on. This system of doubling in the woodwinds permits a section of four or five players to do the work of many more. When *Follies* was performed by the New York Philharmonic, for example, seventeen nondoubling woodwind players—four flutes, four clarinets, a bass clarinet, an oboe, an English horn, a bassoon, and five saxophones—were required to execute the parts written for five doublers. The woodwinds—the quirky, temperamental prima donnas of the orchestra—are the most difficult to write for, but they provide essential color and personality to the orchestra and are well worth the trouble.

Three horns were employed. Such a large section is unusual in musicals, although Don Walker used three in *The Most Happy Fella* and *She Loves Me,* as did Russell Bennett in *South Pacific* and *The King and I.* They give an elegant, rounded middle to the ensemble, as well as a brilliant unison in *forte* passages such as my rather blatant quotation from *Der Rosenkavalier* in "A Weekend in the Country."

The brass section consists of two trumpets and a single trombone. Although they are little heard from, they make themselves valuable in the full *tuttis* as well as various mock-military effects (mostly involving Carl-Magnus) and coloristic passages such as the chattering trumpets in "Now." At one period during tryouts there were so few notes in the trombone part (I once counted them at 113) that the instrument was in danger of losing its place in the orchestra. I had this problem in mind as I approached my next assignment, "It Would Have Been Wonderful." Fortunately the number involved the strutting dragoon Carl-Magnus, and I was able to feature the trombone in a solo *obbligato,* making the instrument indispensable and thereby saving its job, for which it has never thanked me.

Although the presence of a piano is dictated by both the score and the script, being necessary to portray Fredrika's piano exercises, the instrument has no place in this type of orchestra and aside from these passages remains tacet, taking no part in the orchestration. The pianist doubles on the celesta, which is liberally used, due to its charming, bell-like tone. The harp, with its intense romantic associations, was assigned an elaborate and necessarily difficult part, particularly complex for the harpist in that the highly chromatic nature of the score requires a virtual tap dance among the pedals that provide the sharps and flats. The harp figures prominently as an accompanying instrument, so evocative of the romantic past and far more idiomatic than the commonplace piano or the homely guitar.

The strings form the most important element of the *Night Music* orchestra, although the minimum of twenty-five players restricted me to six violins, two violas, two 'cellos, and a bass, which is what we laughingly refer to on Broadway as a full string section. Generations of theater orchestrators, however, have over the years developed an arsenal of trick voicings, mostly unknown to classical composers, in order to achieve a fuller resonance from their skimpy string sections. It is customary to double the number of strings in the orchestra for cast recordings, so that the string sound that one hears on cast albums is far richer, sometimes to a fault, than what one hears from the pit.

In Broadway show orchestration, and commercial work in general, string writing is pretty much confined to the following:

1. Melody and countermelody, unison or harmonized
2. Sustained harmonic accompaniment ("footballs")
3. Runs, trills, tremolos, and other decoration
4. The ubiquitous afterbeats, so abhorred by players.

The score demanded more ambitious use of the string group, particularly for rhythmic accompaniment passages, due to the absence of a rhythm section. It was necessary to draw upon my studies of classical and modern music in order to employ such devices as *pizzicato, spiccato,* double and triple stopping, and harmonics, which permitted a wider and more flexible use of the strings as background. They replaced the customary but inappropriate pianos, guitars, and other rhythm instruments, for which I am greatly indebted to Debussy, Mahler, Bartók, and Stravinsky.

Customarily the units of the string group (violins, violas, 'cellos) play in unison. In addition to this necessary *tutti* writing, I call for an unusual (for Broadway) number of *divisi* passages as well as solos for the violin, 'cello, and even the viola, and occasional duets and trios for solo string instruments. The 'cello *obbligato* in "Later" stands out, as does the gypsy-like violin solo at the very end of the show—a chromatic scale, quite awkward for the violin, climbing to an *altissimo* E natural. Of all the violinists that I have heard attempt it, none played it better than the toupeed contractor of the tryout orchestra in Boston.

Sondheim's original concept was of a dark, somewhat Chekhovian, yet romantic and erotic musical taking the form of a theme and variations, the first act forming the theme and the second the variations. This idea was to take shape as a farce at the country house, using the device of Madame Armfeldt's dealing the cards each time the plot went wrong, and starting again. Wheeler's book, however, did not support this notion, and some of the darker elements of Sondheim's score were replaced during the rehearsal period by lighter material. Such numbers as "Bang!" and "My Husband the Pig" gave way to the more easygoing "In Praise of Women" and "Every Day a Little Death."

Due to the extensive rewriting required by this change of tone in the show, Sondheim fell behind in his writing schedule and rehearsals had to begin before the score was completed. Sondheim is a systematic, skillful writer, and as rehearsals proceeded such material as the "Night Waltzes," "In Praise of Women," "Every Day a Little Death," "It Would Have Been Wonderful," and "A Weekend in the Country" arrived, and, finally, "Send in the Clowns."

Sondheim finds the amazing success of this song, though most welcome, a little baffling. Most of his shows, he says, have at least one simple romantic ballad, but none of these had received what seems to him the disproportionate acclamation attracted by what he refers to as a *boîte* song. Perhaps its appeal lies to some degree in the fact that it is written in short phrases in order to be acted rather than sung; in fact, it was tailor-made to suit the abilities of Glynis Johns, who lacks the vocal power to sustain long phrases, and the song does not actually work very well when sung "correctly" by a trained singer.

"Send in the Clowns" was orchestrated overnight in a hotel room in Boston in between orchestra rehearsals. The orchestration for strings, harp, and solo clarinet is quite conventional, and most of the night was spent in deciding between the solo clarinet and 'cello to play the now familiar unaccompanied introduction and the subsequent *obbligato*. I chose the clarinet for its haunting, lonely effect in its low register and rejected the 'cello, which I felt was too closely associated with another character, Henrik. The reprise is scored for the full orchestra in what I refer to as the "Max Steiner" section, a most gratifying romantic climax in the honored Hollywood tradition. It sounds even better in the movie, with three trombones.

Bobby Short heard the song in Boston, fell in love with it, and asked for a copy. Soon he was performing it in New York, where Judy Collins heard it and invited me to record it with her as orchestrator-conductor. The recording orchestration that I prepared for Judy substituted an English horn for the clarinet, but is otherwise similar to that used in the show. The record soared, providing Sondheim with his biggest hit to date.

A Little Night Music has taken its place among the classics of the musical theater, the most popular, along with *A Funny Thing Happened on the Way to the Forum* and *Sweeney Todd,* of Sondheim's works. It won for its authors a brace of Tony awards, and the cast album has become a staple in the collections of all lovers of musicals. It is a witty and well-constructed work that embraces and uplifts its audience in an atmosphere of warmth and romantic good nature. There is no better example of Sondheim's penchant for an erudite, knowing, whimsical chuckle at the human condition.

Jonathan Tunick

New York
September 1990

Victoria Mallory (Anne Egerman), Garn Stephens (Petra, but replaced prior to the Broadway opening by D. Jamin-Bartlett), George Lee Andrews (Frid), Laurence Guittard (Count Carl-Magnus Malcolm), Patricia Elliott (Countess Charlotte Malcolm), Len Cariou (Fredrik Egerman), Glynis Johns (Desirée Armfeldt) and Hermione Gingold (Madame Armfeldt)

A Little Night Music

CAST OF CHARACTERS

MADAME ARMFELDT
DESIRÉE ARMFELDT, *her daughter, an actress*
FREDRIKA ARMFELDT, *Desirée's daughter*
FREDRIK EGERMAN, *a lawyer*
ANNE EGERMAN, *his second wife*
HENRIK EGERMAN, *his son*
COUNT CARL-MAGNUS MALCOLM, *a dragoon*
COUNTESS CHARLOTTE MALCOLM, *his wife*
PETRA, *the Egerman maid*
FRID, *Madame Armfeldt's butler*
MALLA, *Desirée's maid*
BERTRAND, *Madame Armfeldt's page*
OSA, *Madame Armfeldt's maid*
MR. LINDQUIST
MRS. NORDSTROM
MRS. ANDERSSEN
MR. ERLANSON
MRS. SEGSTROM

MUSICAL NUMBERS

Overture	MR. LINDQUIST, MRS. NORDSTROM, MRS. ANDERSSEN, MR. ERLANSON, MRS. SEGSTROM

ACT I

"Night Waltz"	COMPANY
"Now"	FREDRIK
"Later"	HENRIK
"Soon"	ANNE, HENRIK, FREDRIK
"The Glamorous Life"	FREDRIKA, DESIRÉE, MALLA, MADAME ARMFELDT, MRS. NORDSTROM, MRS. SEGSTROM, MRS. ANDERSSEN, MR. LINDQUIST, MR. ERLANSON
"Remember?"	MR. LINDQUIST, MRS. NORDSTROM, MRS. SEGSTROM, MR. ERLANSON, MRS. ANDERSSEN
"You Must Meet My Wife"	FREDRIK, DESIRÉE
"Liaisons"	MADAME ARMFELDT
"In Praise of Women"	CARL-MAGNUS
"Every Day a Little Death"	CHARLOTTE, ANNE
"A Weekend in the Country"	COMPANY

ACT II

"The Sun Won't Set"	MRS. ANDERSSEN, MRS. SEGSTROM, MRS. NORDSTROM, MR. LINDQUIST, MR. ERLANSON
"It Would Have Been Wonderful"	FREDRIK, CARL-MAGNUS
"Night Waltz II"	MRS. NORDSTROM, MR. ERLANSON, MR. LINDQUIST, MRS. SEGSTROM, MRS. ANDERSSEN
"Perpetual Anticipation"	MRS. NORDSTROM, MRS. SEGSTROM, MRS. ANDERSSEN
"Send in the Clowns"	DESIRÉE
"The Miller's Son"	PETRA
Finale	COMPANY

17

Time: Turn of the Century
Place: Sweden

Overture

Before the houselights are down, MR. LINDQUIST *appears and sits at the piano. He removes his gloves, plunks a key, and begins to vocalize.* MRS. NORDSTROM *enters, hits a key on the piano, and vocalizes with him.* MRS. ANDERSSEN, MR. ERLANSON *and* MRS. SEGSTROM *come out and join the vocalizing.*

MEN:	WOMEN:
La, la la la	La, la la la
La, la la la	La, la la la

MRS. NORDSTROM:
  The old deserted beach that we walked —
  Remember?

MR. ERLANSON:
  Remember?
  The café in the park where we talked —
  Remember?

MRS. ANDERSSEN:
  Remember?
  The tenor on the boat that we chartered,
  Belching "The Bartered
  Bride" —

19

ALL:

Ah, how we laughed,
Ah, how we cried,

MR. LINDQUIST:
Ah, how you promised
And
Ah, how
I lied.

OTHER MEMBERS OF QUINTET:
La, la la la

Ah . . .
Lie . . . lie . . . lie . . .

MRS. SEGSTROM:

That dilapidated inn —
Remember, darling?

MR. ERLANSON:

The proprietress's grin,
Also her glare.

MRS. NORDSTROM:

Yellow gingham on the bed —
Remember, darling?

MR. LINDQUIST:

And the canopy in red,
Needing repair.

ALL:

Soon, I promise.
Soon I won't shy away,
Dear old —
Soon. I want to.
Soon, whatever you say.
Even

WOMEN:
Now,
When we're close and
We

MEN:
Now, when we touch,

20

Touch,
And you're kissing my
Brow,
I don't mind it
Too much.
And you'll have to

Touching my brow,

Ahhhh . . .

ALL:

Admit I'm endearing,
I help keep things humming,
I'm not domineering,
What's one small shortcoming?

And

Unpack the luggage, la la la
Pack up the luggage, la la la
Unpack the luggage, la la la
Hi-ho, the glamorous life!

Unpack the luggage, la la la
Pack up the luggage, la la la
Unpack the luggage, la la la
Hi-ho, the glamorous life!

MR. LINDQUIST:
Ahhhhh . . .

OTHER MEMBERS OF QUINTET:
Unpack the luggage, la la la
Pack up the luggage, la la la

MRS. NORDSTROM:
Ahhhh . . .

OTHER MEMBERS OF QUINTET:
Unpack the luggage, la la la
Hi-ho, the glamorous life!

ALL:

Bring up the curtain, la la la
Bring down the curtain, la la la
Bring up the curtain, la la la
Hi-ho, hi-ho
For the glamorous life!

21

(After the applause, the QUINTET *starts to waltz. The show curtain flies out revealing the main characters doing a strangely surreal waltz [*"Night Waltz"*] of their own, in which partners change partners and recouple with others. The* QUINTET *drifts up into the waltzing couples, and reappears to hum accompaniment for the last section of the dance.* FREDRIKA *wanders through the waltz, too, watching)*

ACT I

Prologue

At the end of the opening waltz, MADAME ARMFELDT *is brought on in her wheelchair by her butler,* FRID. *In her lap is a tray containing a silver cigarette box, a small vase with four yellow bud-roses, and the cards with which she is playing solitaire. She is watched by* FREDRIKA ARMFELDT, *13 — a grave, very self-contained and formal girl with the precise diction of the convent-trained.*

FREDRIKA: If you cheated a little, it would come out.

MADAME ARMFELDT (*Continuing to play*): Solitaire is the only thing in life that demands absolute honesty. As a woman who has numbered kings among her lovers, I think my word can be taken on that point.
(*She motions to* FRID, *who crosses down and lights her cigarette*)
What was I talking about?

FREDRIKA: You said I should watch.

MADAME ARMFELDT: Watch — what?

FREDRIKA: It sounds very unlikely to me, but you said I should watch for the night to smile.

MADAME ARMFELDT: Everything is unlikely, dear, so don't let

that deter you. Of course the summer night smiles. Three times.

FREDRIKA: But how does it smile?

MADAME ARMFELDT: Good heavens, what sort of nanny did you have?

FREDRIKA: None, really. Except Mother, and the other actresses in the company — and the stage manager.

MADAME ARMFELDT: Stage managers are not nannies. They don't have the talent.

FREDRIKA: But if it happens — how does it happen?

MADAME ARMFELDT: You get a feeling. Suddenly the jasmine starts to smell stronger, then a frog croaks — then all the stars in Orion wink. Don't squeeze your bosoms against the chair, dear. It'll stunt their growth. And then where would you be?

FREDRIKA: But why does it smile, Grandmother?

MADAME ARMFELDT: At the follies of human beings, of course. The first smile smiles at the young, who know nothing.
(*She looks pointedly at* FREDRIKA)
The second, at the fools who know too little, like Desirée.

FREDRIKA: Mother isn't a fool.

MADAME ARMFELDT (*Going right on*): Um-hum. And the third at the old who know too much — like me.
(*The game is over without coming out. Annoyed at the cards,* MADAME ARMFELDT *scatters them at random, and barks at* FRID)
Frid, time for my nap.

FREDRIKA (*Intrigued in spite of herself, gazes out at the summer night*): Grandmother, might it really smile tonight?

MADAME ARMFELDT: Why not? Now, practice your piano, dear, preferably with the soft pedal down. And as a treat tonight at dinner, I shall tell you amusing stories about my liaison with the Baron de Signac, who was, to put it mildly, peculiar.

(FRID *wheels her off and* FREDRIKA *goes to sit at the piano*)

Scene 1

THE EGERMAN ROOMS

Two rooms: the parlor and the master bedroom, indicated on different levels. ANNE EGERMAN, *a ravishingly pretty girl of 18, is on the bed. She goes to the vanity table, toys with her hair, and then enters the parlor.* HENRIK EGERMAN, *her stepson, a brooding young man of 19, is seated on the sofa, playing his cello. Beside him on the sofa is a book with a ribbon marker.* ANNE *looks at* HENRIK, *then leans over the sofa to get his attention.*

ANNE: Oh Henrik, dear, don't you have anything less gloomy to practice?

HENRIK: It isn't gloomy, it's profound.

ANNE (*Reaches down, takes* HENRIK*'s book, and begins reading from it*): " . . . in discussing temptation, Martin Luther says: 'You cannot prevent the birds from flying over your head, but you can prevent them from nesting in your hair.'" Oh dear, that's gloomy too! Don't they teach you anything at the seminary a little more cheerful?

HENRIK (*Grand*): A man who's going to serve in God's Army must learn all the ruses and stratagems of the Enemy.

ANNE (*Sitting, giggling*): And which of your professors made that historic statement?

HENRIK (*Caught out*): Pastor Ericson, as a matter of fact. He says we're like generals learning to win battles against the devil.
(*Her ball of silk falls off her lap*)

ANNE: Oh dear, my ball!
(HENRIK *bends down to pick up the ball. He stands beside her, obviously overwhelmed by her nearness.* ANNE *pats her lap*)
You can put it there, you know. My lap isn't one of the Devil's snares.
(*Flushing,* HENRIK *drops the ball into her lap and moves away from her*)

HENRIK: Anne, I was wondering — could we go for a walk?

ANNE: Now?

HENRIK: I've so much to tell you. What I've been thinking, and everything.

ANNE: Silly Henrik, don't you realize it's almost tea-time? And I think I hear your father.
(*She rises, puts down the ball of silk*)
I'm sure you've made the most wonderful discoveries about life, and I long to talk, but — later.
(FREDRIK *enters, followed by* PETRA, *21, the charming, easy-going maid*)
Fredrik, dear!

HENRIK (*Mutters to himself*): Later.

ANNE: Look who's come home to us — holier than ever.

FREDRIK: Hello, son. How was the examination?

HENRIK: Well, as a matter of fact . . .

FREDRIK (*Breaking in*): You passed with flying colors, of course.

ANNE: First on the list.

HENRIK (*Trying again*): And Pastor Ericson said . . .

FREDRIK (*Breaking in*): Splendid — you must give us a full report. Later.

ANNE: He'd better be careful or he'll go straight to heaven before he has a chance to save any sinners.

FREDRIK: Don't tease him, dear.

ANNE: Oh, Henrik likes to be teased, don't you, Henrik? Fredrik, do you want your tea now?

FREDRIK: Not now, I think. It's been rather an exhausting day in Court and as we have a long evening ahead of us, I feel a little nap is indicated.
(He produces theater tickets from his pocket)

ANNE (*Grabbing at them, delighted as a child*): Tickets for the theater!

FREDRIK: It's a French comedy. I thought it might entertain you.

ANNE: It's *Woman of the World*, isn't it? With Desirée Armfeldt! She's on all the posters! Oh, Fredrik, how delicious!
(To HENRIK, *teasing*)
What shall I wear? My blue with the feathers —
(FREDRIK *pours water*)
genuine angel's feathers — ? Or the yellow? Ah, I know. My pink, with the bosom. And Henrik, you can do me up in the back.
(She goes into the bedroom)

FREDRIK: I'm sorry, son. I should have remembered you were coming home and got a third ticket. But then perhaps a French comedy is hardly suitable.

(FREDRIK *takes a pill*)

HENRIK (*Outburst*): Why does everyone laugh at me? Is it so ridiculous to want to do some good in this world?

FREDRIK: I'm afraid being young in itself can be a trifle ridiculous. Good has to be so good, bad so bad. Such superlatives!

HENRIK: But to be old, I suppose, is not ridiculous.

FREDRIK (*Sigh*): Ah, let's not get into that. I love you very much, you know. So does Anne — in her way. But you can't expect her to take your mother's place. She's young too; she has not yet learned . . .

HENRIK: . . . to suffer fools gladly?

FREDRIK (*Gentle*): You said that, son. Not I.

ANNE: Fredrik!

(*As* FREDRIK *moves into the bedroom,* HENRIK *picks up his book and reads.* ANNE *is sitting on the bed, buffing her nails*)

You were sweet to think of the theater for me.

FREDRIK: I'll enjoy it too.

ANNE: Who wouldn't — when all the posters call her The One And Only Desirée Armfeldt?

(FREDRIK *begins to try to kiss her. She rattles on*)

I wonder what it would feel like to be a One and Only! The One and Only — Anne Egerman!

(*She leaves* FREDRIK *on the bed and moves to the vanity table. As aware as he is of her rejection*)

Poor Fredrik! Do I still make you happy? After eleven months? I know I'm foolish to be so afraid — and you've been so patient, but, soon — I promise. Oh, I know you think I'm too silly to worry, but I do . . .

(As FREDRIK *looks up to answer, she gives a little cry*)
Oh no! For heaven's sakes, can that be a pimple coming?
(FREDRIK, *deflated, begins to sing as he undresses*)

FREDRIK:

Now, as the sweet imbecilities
Tumble so lavishly
Onto her lap . . .

ANNE: Oh Fredrik, what a day it's been! Unending drama!
While Petra was brushing my hair, the doorbell . . .
(*Throughout the song, she continues chattering in pan-
tomime when not actually speaking*)

FREDRIK:

Now, there are two possibilities:
A, I could ravish her,
B, I could nap.

ANNE: . . . that grumpy old Mrs. Nordstrom from next door.
Her sister's coming for a visit . . .

FREDRIK:

Say it's the ravishment, then we see
The option
That follows, of course:

ANNE: . . . do hope I'm imperious enough with the servants.
I try to be. But half the time I think they're laughing at
me . . .

FREDRIK:

A, the deployment of charm, or B,
The adoption
Of physical force.

Now B might arouse her,
But if I assume
I trip on my trouser
Leg crossing the room . . .

Her hair getting tangled,
Her stays getting snapped,
My nerves will be jangled,
My energy sapped . . .

Removing her clothing
Would take me all day
And her subsequent loathing
Would turn me away —
Which eliminates B
And which leaves us with A.

ANNE: Could you ever be jealous of me? . . .

FREDRIK:

Now, insofar as approaching it,
What would be festive
But have its effect?

ANNE: Shall I learn Italian? I think it would be amusing, if
the verbs aren't too irregular . . .

FREDRIK:

Now, there are two ways of broaching it:
A, the suggestive
And B, the direct.

ANNE: . . . but then French is a much chic-er language. Everyone says so. Parlez-vous Français? . . .

FREDRIK:

Say that I settle on B, to wit,
A charmingly
Lecherous mood . . .

A, I could put on my nightshirt or sit
Disarmingly,
B, in the nude . . .
That might be effective,

My body's all right,
But not in perspective
And not in the light . . .

I'm bound to be chilly
And feel a buffoon,
But nightshirts are silly
In midafternoon . . .

Which leaves the suggestive,
But how to proceed?
Although she gets restive,
Perhaps I could read . . .

In view of her penchant
For something romantic,
De Sade is too trenchant
And Dickens too frantic,
And Stendhal would ruin
The plan of attack,
As there isn't much blue in
The Red and the Black.

De Maupassant's candor
Would cause her dismay.
The Brontës are grander
But not very gay.
Her taste is much blander,
I'm sorry to say,
But is Hans Christian Ander-
Sen ever risqué?
Which eliminates A.

(*Exits upstage*)

ANNE: And he said, "You're such a pretty lady!" Wasn't that silly? . . .

FREDRIK (*As he walks back on in nothing but his long underwear*):
Now, with my mental facilities

34

Partially muddied
And ready to snap . . .

ANNE (*At the jewel box now*): . . . I'm sure about the bracelet.
But earrings, earrings! *Which* earrings? . . .

FREDRIK:
Now, though there are possibilities
Still to be studied,
I might as well nap . . .

ANNE: Mother's rubies? . . . Oh, the diamonds are — Agony!
I know . . .

FREDRIK (*Getting into bed*):
Bow though I must
To adjust
My original plan . . .

ANNE: Desirée Armfeldt — I just know she'll wear the most
glamorous gowns! . . .

FREDRIK:
How shall I sleep
Half as deep
As I usually can? . . .

ANNE: Dear, distinguished old Fredrik!

FREDRIK:
When now I still want and/or love you,
Now, as always,
Now,
Anne?
    (FREDRIK *turns over and goes to sleep. They remain frozen.*
    PETRA *enters the parlor*)

PETRA: Nobody rang. Doesn't he want his tea?

HENRIK (*Still deep in book*): They're taking a nap.

PETRA (*Coming up behind him, teasingly ruffling his hair*): You
smell of soap.

HENRIK (*Pulling his head away*): I'm reading.

PETRA (*Caressing his head*): Do those old teachers take a scrubbing brush to you every morning and scrub you down like a dray horse?

(*Strokes his ear*)

HENRIK (*Fierce*): Get away from me!

PETRA (*Jumping up in mock alarm*): Oh what a wicked woman I am! I'll go straight to hell!

(*Starting away, she goes toward the door, deliberately wiggling her hips*)

HENRIK (*Looking up, even fiercer*): And don't walk like that!

PETRA (*Innocent*): Like — what?

(*Wiggles even more*)

Like this?

HENRIK (*Pleadingly*): Stop it. Stop it!

(*He rises, goes after her, clutches her, and starts savagely, clumsily, to kiss her and fumble at her breasts. She slaps his hand*)

PETRA: Careful!

(*Breaks away*)

That's a new blouse! A whole week's wages and the lace extra!

(*Looks at him*)

Poor little Henrik!

(*Then affectionately pats his cheek*)

Later! You'll soon get the knack of it!

(*She exits.* HENRIK *puts down the book, gets his cello and begins to sing, accompanying himself on the cello*)

HENRIK:

Later . . .

When is later? . . .

All you ever hear is "Later, Henrik! Henrik, later . . . "

"Yes, we know, Henrik.
Oh, Henrik —
Everyone agrees, Henrik —
Please, Henrik!"
You have a thought you're fairly bursting with,
A personal discovery or problem, and it's
"What's your rush, Henrik?
Shush, Henrik —
Goodness, how you gush, Henrik —
Hush, Henrik!"
You murmur,
"I only . . .
It's just that . . .
For God's sake!"
"Later, Henrik . . . "

"Henrik" . . .
Who is "Henrik"? . . .
Oh, that lawyer's son, the one who mumbles —
Short and boring,
Yes, he's hardly worth ignoring
And who cares if he's all dammed —
                    (*Looks up*)
— I beg your pardon —
Up inside?
As I've
Often stated,
It's intolerable
Being tolerated.
"Reassure Henrik,
Poor Henrik.
Henrik, you'll endure
Being pure, Henrik."

Though I've been born, I've never been!
How can I wait around for later?

I'll be ninety on my deathbed
And the late, or rather later,
Henrik Egerman!

Doesn't anything begin?
> (ANNE, *in the bedroom, gets up from the vanity table and stands near the bed, singing to* FREDRIK)

ANNE:
Soon, I promise.
Soon I won't shy away,
Dear old —
> (*She bites her lip*)

Soon. I want to.
Soon, whatever you say.
Even now,
When you're close and we touch,
And you're kissing my brow,
I don't mind it too much.
And you'll have to admit
I'm endearing,
I help keep things humming,
I'm not domineering,
What's one small shortcoming?
And think of how I adore you,
Think of how much you love me.
If I were perfect for you,
Wouldn't you tire of me
Soon,
All too soon?
Dear old —
> (*The sound of* HENRIK's *cello.* FREDRIK *stirs noisily in bed.* ANNE *goes into the parlor*)

Henrik! That racket! Your father's sleeping!
> (*She remains, half-innocent, half-coquettish, in her negligee. For a second,* ANNE *watches him. She closes her nightgown at the neck and goes back into the bedroom*)

ANNE (*Back at the bed*):
  Soon —

HENRIK:
  "Later" . . .

ANNE:
  I promise.

HENRIK:
  When is "later?"
                    (*Simultaneously*)

ANNE: HENRIK:
Soon   "Later, Henrik, later."
I won't shy   All you ever hear is,
Away,   "Yes, we know, Henrik, oh,
                                     Henrik,
Dear old —   Everyone agrees, Henrik,
                                     please, Henrik!"
           (FREDRIK *stirs. Simultaneously*)

ANNE:
Soon.   HENRIK: FREDRIK:
I want to.   "Later" . . .   Now,
                 When is "later"?   As the sweet
                                         imbecilities
                 All you ever   Trip on my trouser leg,

Soon,
                 Hear is
Whatever you
Say.   "Later, Henrik,
                                     Stendhal
                                         eliminates
                 Later."   A,
                 As I've often
                 Stated: But
                 When?   When?

39

Even	Maybe	Maybe
Now,		
When you're close	Soon, soon	Later.
And we touch	I'll be ninety	
	And	
And you're kissing	Dead.	When I'm kissing
My brow,		Your brow
I don't mind it	I don't mind it	And I'm stroking
		your head,
Too much,	Too much,	
		You'll come into
		my bed.
And you'll have	Since I have to	And you have to
to admit	Admit	Admit
I'm endearing,	I find peering	I've been hearing
I help		
Keep things	Through life's	All those tremu-
		lous cries
Humming, I'm	Gray windows	
	Impatiently	Patiently,
Not domineering,	Not very cheering.	Not interfering
What's one small	Do I fear death?	With those tremu-
		lous thighs.
Shortcoming?	Let it	
And	Come to me	Come to me
Think of how	Now,	Soon,
I adore you,		
Think of how	Now,	Soon,
Much you love me.		
If I were perfect	Now,	Soon,
For you,		
Wouldn't you tire	Now.	Soon.
Of me		
Later?	Come to me	Come to me
	Soon. If I'm	Soon,

```
                    Dead,
We will,            I can
Later.              Wait.           Straight to me,
                                      never mind
                    How can I       How.
We will . . .       Live until      Darling,
Soon.               Later?          Now —
                                    I still want and/or
                    Later . . .     Love
                                    You,

Soon.                               Now, as
                    Later . . .     Always,
Soon.                               Now,
                                      (He does a kiss)
                                    Desirée.
```

(ANNE *stares out, astonished, as the lights go down and the bedroom and parlor roll off.* FREDRIKA, *still at the piano, is playing scales*)

FREDRIKA (*Sings*):
Ordinary mothers lead ordinary lives:
Keep the house and sweep the parlor,
Cook the meals and look exhausted.
Ordinary mothers, like ordinary wives,
Fry the eggs and dry the sheets and
Try to deal with facts.

Mine acts.
(DESIRÉE *sweeps on with* MALLA, *her maid, in tow.* MALLA *carries a wig box, suitcase, and parasol*)

DESIRÉE (*As* FREDRIKA *reads a letter from her*):
Darling, I miss you a lot
But, darling, this has to be short
As Mother is getting a plaque
From the Halsingborg Arts Council

41

Amateur Theatre Group.
Whether it's funny or not,
I'll give you a fuller report
The minute they carry me back
From the Halsingborg Arts Council
Amateur Theatre Group . . .
Love you . . .

(*The* QUINTET *appears*)

QUINTET:
Unpack the luggage, la la la
Pack up the luggage, la la la
Unpack the luggage, la la la
Hi-ho, the glamorous life!

MRS. SEGSTROM:
Ice in the basin, la la la

MR. ERLANSON:
Cracks in the plaster, la la la

MRS. ANDERSSEN:
Mice in the hallway, la la la

ALL THE QUINTET:
Hi-ho, the glamorous life!

MEN:
Run for the carriage, la la la

WOMEN:
Wolf down the sandwich, la la la

ALL THE QUINTET:
Which town is this one? La la la
Hi-ho, the glamorous life!

(FRID *wheels* MADAME ARMFELDT *onstage*)

MADAME ARMFELDT:
Ordinary daughters ameliorate their lot,

Use their charms and choose their futures,
Breed their children, heed their mothers.
Ordinary daughters, which mine, I fear, is not,
Tend each asset, spend it wisely
While it still endures . . .

Mine tours.

DESIRÉE (*As* MADAME ARMFELDT *reads a letter from her*):
Mother, forgive the delay,
My schedule is driving me wild.
But, Mother, I really must run,
I'm performing in Rottvik,
And don't ask where is it, please.
How are you feeling today
And are you corrupting the child?
Don't. Mother, the minute I'm done
With performing in Rottvik,
I'll come for a visit

And argue.

MEN:
Mayors with speeches, la la la

WOMEN:
Children with posies, la la la

MEN:
Half-empty houses, la la la

ALL THE QUINTET:
Hi-ho, the glamorous life!

MRS. NORDSTROM:
Cultural lunches,

ALL THE QUINTET:
La la la

43

MRS. ANDERSSEN:
Dead floral tributes,

ALL THE QUINTET:
La la la

MR. LINDQUIST:
Ancient admirers,

ALL THE QUINTET:
La la la
Hi-ho, the glamorous life!

FREDRIKA:
Mother's romantic, la la la

MADAME ARMFELDT:
Mother's misguided, la la la

DESIRÉE:
Mother's surviving, la la la
Leading the glamorous life!
    (*Holds up a mirror*)
Cracks in the plaster, la la la
Youngish admirers, la la la
Which one was that one? La la la
Hi-ho, the glamorous life!

DESIRÉE *and* QUINTET:
Bring up the curtain, la la la
Bring down the curtain, la la la
Bring up the curtain, la la la
Hi-ho, the glamorous . . .
Life.

Scene 2

STAGE OF LOCAL THEATER

The show curtain is down. Two stage boxes are visible. Sitting in one are MR. LINDQUIST, MRS. NORDSTROM, *and* MR. ERLANSON. ANNE *and* FREDRIK *enter, and speak as they walk to their box.*

ANNE: Does she look like her pictures?

FREDRIK: Who, dear?

ANNE: Desirée Armfeldt, of course.

FREDRIK: How would I know, dear?

ANNE (*Pause*): I only thought . . .

FREDRIK: You only thought — what?

ANNE: Desirée is not a common name. I mean, none of your typists and things are called Desirée, are they?

FREDRIK: My typists and things in descending order of importance are Miss Osa Svensen, Miss Ona Nilsson, Miss Gerda Bjornson, *and* Mrs. Amalia Lindquist.
    (*A* PAGE *enters, and knocks three times with the staff he is carrying. The show curtain rises revealing the stage*

behind it, a tatty Louis XIV "salon," as PAGE *exits. For a moment it is empty. Then two* LADIES, *in rather shabby court costumes, enter*)

FIRST LADY (MRS. SEGSTROM): Tell me something about this remarkable Countess, Madame.

SECOND LADY (MRS. ANDERSSEN): I shall try as best I can to depict the personality of the Countess, Madame, although it is too rich in mysterious contradictions to be described in a few short moments.

FIRST LADY: It is said that her power over men is most extraordinary.

SECOND LADY: There is a great deal of truth in that, Madame, and her lovers are as many as the pearls in the necklace which she always wears.

FIRST LADY: Your own husband, Madame, is supposed to be one of the handsomest pearls, is he not?

SECOND LADY: He fell in love with the Countess on sight. She took him as a lover for three months and after that I had him back.

FIRST LADY: And your marriage was crushed?

SECOND LADY: On the contrary, Madame! My husband had become a tender, devoted, admirable lover, a faithful husband and an exemplary father. The Countess's lack of decency is most moral.

(*The* PAGE *re-enters*)

PAGE: The Countess Celimène de Francen de la Tour de Casa.

(*The* COUNTESS — DESIRÉE — *makes her sensational entrance. A storm of applause greets her.* FREDRIK *claps.* ANNE *does not as she glares at the stage. During the applause,* DESIRÉE *makes a deep curtsey, during which, old pro that*

46

she is, she cases the house. Her eye falls on FREDRIK. *She does a take and instantly all action freezes*)

MR. LINDQUIST (*Sings*):
  Remember?

MRS. NORDSTROM (*Sings*):
  Remember?
      (MR. LINDQUIST *and* MRS. NORDSTROM *leave the stage box*)
  The old deserted beach that we walked —
  Remember?

MR. LINDQUIST:
  Remember?
  The café in the park where we talked —
  Remember?

MRS. NORDSTROM:
  Remember?

MR. LINDQUIST:
  The tenor on the boat that we chartered,
  Belching "The Bartered
  Bride" —

BOTH:
  Ah, how we laughed,
  Ah, how we cried.

MR. LINDQUIST:
  Ah, how you promised and
  Ah, how I lied.

MRS. NORDSTROM:
  That dilapidated inn —
  Remember, darling?

MR. LINDQUIST:
  The proprietress's grin,
  Also her glare . . .

47

MRS. NORDSTROM:
 Yellow gingham on the bed —
 Remember, darling?

MR. LINDQUIST:
 And the canopy in red,
 Needing repair?

BOTH:
 I *think* you were there.
  (*They return to the stage box and the action continues*)

ANNE (*Fierce, to* FREDRIK): She looked at us. Why did she look at us?

DESIRÉE (*To* SECOND LADY): Dear Madame Merville, what a charming mischance to find you here this evening.

FREDRIK: I don't think she looked especially at us.

ANNE:	SECOND LADY:
She did! She peered, then she smiled.	Charming, indeed, dear Celimène.

SECOND LADY: May I be permitted to present my school friend from the provinces? Madame Vilmorac — whose husband, I'm sure, is in dire need of a little expert polishing.

FIRST LADY: Oh, dear Countess, you are all but a legend to me. I implore you to reveal to me the secret of your success with the hardier sex!

ANNE: She smiled at us!
  (*Grabs* FREDRIK*'s opera glasses and studies the stage*)

DESIRÉE: Dear Madame, that can be summed up in a single word —

ANNE: She's ravishingly beautiful.

FREDRIK: Make-up.

DESIRÉE: — dignity.

TWO LADIES: Dignity?

ANNE (*Turning on* FREDRIK): How can you be sure — if you've never seen her?

FREDRIK: Hush!

DESIRÉE (*Playing her first-act set speech*): Dignity. We women have a right to commit any crime toward our husbands, our lovers, our sons, as long as we do not hurt their dignity. We should make men's dignity our best ally and caress it, cradle it, speak tenderly to it, and handle it as our most delightful toy. Then a man is in our hands, at our feet, or anywhere else we momentarily wish him to be.

ANNE (*Sobbing*):   FREDRIK:
I want to go home!   Anne!

ANNE: I want to go home!

FREDRIK: Anne!
> (*She runs off,* FREDRIK *following*)

Scene 3

THE EGERMAN ROOMS

In the parlor, PETRA, *lying on the couch, is calmly re-arranging her blouse.* HENRIK, *in a storm of tension, is pulling on his trousers. On the floor beside them is a bottle of champagne and two glasses.*

HENRIK: We have sinned, and it was a complete failure!
> (*Struggling with his fly buttons*)
These buttons, these insufferable buttons!

PETRA: Here, dear, let me.
> (*She crosses, kneels in front of him, and starts to do up the fly buttons*)
Don't you worry, little Henrik. Just let it rest a while.
> (*She pats his fly*)
There. Now you put on your sweater and do a nice little quiet bit of reading.
> (*She gets his sweater from the back of a chair and helps him into it.* ANNE *enters, still crying. She sees* HENRIK *and* PETRA, *lets out a sob, and runs into the bedroom.* FREDRIK *enters. Perfectly calm, to* FREDRIK)
My, that was a short play.

FREDRIK: My wife became ill; I had to bring her home.

(*He gives* HENRIK *a look, sizing up the situation approvingly, before following* ANNE *into the bedroom*)

Anne!

    (HENRIK *starts again toward* PETRA, *who avoids him*)

PETRA: No, lamb. I told you. Give it a nice rest and you'll be surprised how perky it'll be by morning.

    (*She wiggles her way out.* FREDRIK *has now entered the bedroom;* ANNE *is no longer visible — as if she had moved into an inner room. In the parlor,* HENRIK *picks up the champagne bottle and glasses and puts them on the table*)

ANNE (*Off, calling*): Fredrik!

FREDRIK: Yes, dear.

ANNE: Did you have many women between your first wife and me? Sometimes when I think of what memories you have, I vanish inside.

FREDRIK: Before I met you I was quite a different man. Many things were different. Better?

    (ANNE *comes back into the bedroom*)

Worse? Different, anyway.

ANNE: Do you remember when I was a little girl and you came to my father's house for dinner and told me fairy tales? Do you remember?

FREDRIK: Yes, I remember.

ANNE (*Sitting on* FREDRIK's *lap*): Then you were "Uncle Fredrik" and now you're my husband. Isn't that amusing? You were so lonely and sad that summer. I felt terribly sorry for you, so I said: "Poor thing, I'll marry him." Are you coming to bed yet?

FREDRIK: Not just yet. I think I'll go for a breath of fresh air.

ANNE: That wasn't an amusing play, was it?

FREDRIK: We didn't see that much of it.

ANNE: I wonder how old that Armfeldt woman can be. At least fifty — don't you think?

FREDRIK: I wouldn't say that old.

ANNE: Well, goodnight.

FREDRIK: Goodnight.
> (*As* FREDRIK *moves into the parlor,* MR. LINDQUIST *and* MRS. NORDSTROM *appear. There is a musical sting and* FREDRIK *and* HENRIK *freeze*)

MRS. NORDSTROM (*Sings*):
Remember?

MR. LINDQUIST (*Sings*):
Remember?

BOTH:
Remember?
Remember?
> (FREDRIK *unfreezes, clasps his hands together and goes into the parlor.* HENRIK *looks anxiously at his father*)

HENRIK: Is she all right now?

FREDRIK: Oh yes, she's all right.

HENRIK: It wasn't anything serious?

FREDRIK: No, nothing serious.

HENRIK: You don't think — a doctor? I mean, it would be terrible if it was something — serious.

FREDRIK: Pray for her, son. Correction — pray for me. Goodnight.

HENRIK: Goodnight, father.

(FREDRIK *exits, and* MRS. NORDSTROM *and* MR. LINDQUIST
sweep downstage)

MRS. NORDSTROM (*Sings*):
The local village dance on the green —
Remember?

MR. LINDQUIST (*Sings*):
Remember?
The lady with the large tambourine —
Remember?

MRS. NORDSTROM:
Remember?
The one who played the harp in her boa
Thought she was so a-
Dept.

BOTH:
Ah, how we laughed,
Ah, how we wept.
Ah, how we polka'd

MRS. NORDSTROM:
And ah, how we slept.
How we kissed and how we clung —
Remember, darling?

MR. LINDQUIST:
We were foolish, we were young —

BOTH:
More than we knew.

MRS. NORDSTROM:
Yellow gingham on the bed,
Remember, darling?
And the canopy in red —

MR. LINDQUIST:

Or was it blue?

> (MRS. NORDSTROM *and* MR. LINDQUIST *are joined by* MRS.
> SEGSTROM, MRS. ANDERSSEN *and* MR. ERLANSON, *who ap-*
> *pear downstage*)

MRS. SEGSTROM:

The funny little games that we played —
Remember?

MR. ERLANSON:

Remember?
The unexpected knock of the maid —
Remember?

MRS. ANDERSSEN:

Remember?
The wine that made us both rather merry
And, oh, so very
Frank —

ALL:

Ah, how we laughed.
Ah, how we drank.

MR. ERLANSON:

You acquiesced

MRS. ANDERSSEN:

And the rest is a blank.

MR. LINDQUIST:

What we did with your perfume —

MR. ERLANSON:

Remember, darling?

MRS. SEGSTROM:

The condition of the room
When we were through . . .

MRS. NORDSTROM:

Our inventions were unique —
Remember, darling?

MR. LINDQUIST:

I was limping for a week,
You caught the flu . . .

ALL:

I'm *sure* it was —
You.

(They drift off as DESIRÉE*'s digs come on)*

Scene 4

DESIRÉE'S DIGS

> FREDRIK *walks on, as* DESIRÉE, *in a robe, enters, munching a sandwich and carrying a glass of beer.*

FREDRIK: They told me where to find you at the theater.

DESIRÉE: Fredrik!

FREDRIK: Hello, Desirée.
> (*For a moment they gaze at each other*)

DESIRÉE: So it *was* you! I peered and peered and said: "Is it . . . ? Can it be . . . ? Is it possible?" And then, of course, when you walked out after five minutes, I was sure.

FREDRIK: Was my record that bad?

DESIRÉE: Terrible. You walked out on my Hedda in Halsingborg. And on my sensational Phaedra in Ekilstuna.

FREDRIK (*Standing, looking at her*): Fourteen years!

DESIRÉE: Fourteen years!

FREDRIK: No rancor?

DESIRÉE: Rancor? For a while, a little. But now — no rancor, not a trace.

56

(*Indicating a plate of sandwiches*)
Sandwich?

FREDRIK (*Declining*): Hungry as ever after a performance, I see.

DESIRÉE: Worse. I'm a wolf. Sit down.
(*Pouring him a glass of schnapps*)
Here. You never said no to schnapps.
(FREDRIK *sits down on the love seat. She stands, looking at him*)

FREDRIK: About *this* walking out! I'd like to explain.

DESIRÉE: The girl in the pink dress, I imagine.

FREDRIK: You still don't miss a thing, do you?

DESIRÉE: Your wife.

FREDRIK: For the past eleven months. She was so looking forward to the play, she got a little overexcited. She's only eighteen, still almost a child.
(*A pause*)
I'm waiting.

DESIRÉE: For what?

FREDRIK: For you to tell me what an old fool I've become to have fallen under the spell of youth, beginnings, the blank page.
(*Very coolly*, DESIRÉE *opens the robe, revealing her naked body to him*)

DESIRÉE: The page that has been written on — *and* rewritten.

FREDRIK (*Looking, admiring*): With great style. Some things — schnapps, for example — improve with age.

DESIRÉE: Let us hope that proves true of your little bride.
(*She closes the wrapper and stands, still very cool, looking at him*)

57

So you took her home and tucked her up in her cot with her rattle and her woolly penguin.

FREDRIK: Figuratively speaking.

DESIRÉE: And then you came to me.

FREDRIK: I wish you'd ask me why.

DESIRÉE (*Dead pan*): Why did you come to me?

FREDRIK: For old times' sake? For curiosity? To boast about my wife? To complain about her? Perhaps — Hell, why am I being such a lawyer about it?
(*Pause*)
This afternoon when I was taking my nap . . .

DESIRÉE: So you take afternoon naps now!

FREDRIK: Hush! . . . I had the most delightful dream.

DESIRÉE: About . . . ?

FREDRIK: . . . you.

DESIRÉE: Ah! What did we do?

FREDRIK: Well, as a matter of fact, we were in that little hotel in Malmö. We'd been basking in the sun all day.

DESIRÉE (*Suddenly picking it up*): When my back got so burned it was an agony to lie down so you . . . ?

FREDRIK: As vivid as . . . Well, *very* vivid! So you see. My motives for coming here are what might be called — mixed.
(DESIRÉE *suddenly bursts into laughter. Tentative*)
Funny?

DESIRÉE (*Suddenly controlling the laughter, very mock solemn*): No. Not at all.
(*There is a pause, distinctly charged with unadmitted sex*)

FREDRIK (*Looking around, slightly uncomfortable*): How familiar all this is.

58

DESIRÉE: Oh yes, nothing's changed. Uppsala one week. Örebro the next. The same old inevitable routine.

FREDRIK: But it still has its compensations?

DESIRÉE: Yes — no — no — yes.

FREDRIK: That's a rather ambiguous answer.
>   (*Pause*)
You must, at least at times, be lonely.

DESIRÉE (*Smiling*): Dear Fredrik, if you're inquiring about my love life, rest assured. It's quite satisfactory.

FREDRIK: I see. And — if I may ask — at the moment?

DESIRÉE: A dragoon. A very handsome, very married dragoon with, I'm afraid, the vanity of a peacock, the brain of a pea, but the physical proportions . . .

FREDRIK: Don't specify the vegetable, please. I am easily deflated.
>   (*They both burst into spontaneous laughter*)
Oh, Desirée!

DESIRÉE: Fredrik!
>   (*Another charged pause.* FREDRIK *tries again*)

FREDRIK: Desirée, I . . .

DESIRÉE: Yes, dear?

FREDRIK: I — er . . . That is . . .
>   (*Loses his nerve again*)
Perhaps a little more schnapps?

DESIRÉE : Help yourself.
>   (FREDRIK *crosses to the writing desk, where, next to the schnapps, is a framed photograph of* FREDRIKA. *He notices it*)

FREDRIK: Who's this?

DESIRÉE (*Suddenly rather awkward*): That? Oh — my daughter.

FREDRIK: Your daughter? I had no idea . . .

DESIRÉE: She happened.

FREDRIK: She's charming. Where is she now?

DESIRÉE: She's with my mother in the country. She used to tour with me, and then one day Mother swept up like the Wrath of God and saved her from me — You never knew my mother! She always wins *our* battles.
(*Wanting to get off the subject*)
I think perhaps a little schnapps for me too.

FREDRIK: Oh yes, of course.
(FREDRIK *pours a second schnapps. The charged pause again*)

DESIRÉE (*Indicating the room*): I apologize for all this squalor!

FREDRIK: On the contrary, I have always associated you very happily with — chaos.
(*Pause*)
So.

DESIRÉE: So.

FREDRIK (*Artificially bright*): Well, I think it's time to talk about my wife, don't you?

DESIRÉE: Boast or complain?

FREDRIK: Both, I expect.
(*Sings*)
She lightens my sadness,
She livens my days,
She bursts with a kind of madness
My well-ordered ways.
My happiest mistake,
The ache of my life:
You must meet my wife.

She bubbles with pleasure,

60

She glows with surprise,
Disrupts my accustomed leisure
And ruffles my ties.
I don't know even now
Quite how it began.
You must meet my wife, my Anne.

One thousand whims to which I give in,
Since her smallest tear turns me ashen.
I never dreamed that I could live in
So completely demented,
Contented
A fashion.

So sunlike, so winning,
So unlike a wife.
I do think that I'm beginning
To show signs of life.
Don't ask me how at my age
One still can grow —
If you met my wife,
You'd know.

DESIRÉE: Dear Fredrik, I'm just longing to meet her. Sometime.

FREDRIK:
    She sparkles.

DESIRÉE:
    How pleasant.

FREDRIK:
    She twinkles.

DESIRÉE:
    How nice.

FREDRIK:
    Her youth is a sort of present —

DESIRÉE:
Whatever the price.

FREDRIK:
The incandescent — what? — the —

DESIRÉE (*Proffering a cigarette*):
Light?

FREDRIK (*Lighting it*):
— Of my life!
You must meet my wife.

DESIRÉE:
Yes, I must, I really must. Now —

FREDRIK:
She flutters.

DESIRÉE:
How charming.

FREDRIK:
She twitters.

DESIRÉE:
My word!

FREDRIK:
She floats.

DESIRÉE:
Isn't that alarming?
What is she, a bird?

FREDRIK:
She makes me feel I'm — what? —

DESIRÉE:
A very old man?

FREDRIK:
Yes — no!

DESIRÉE:
   No.

FREDRIK:
   But —

DESIRÉE:
   I must meet your Gertrude.

FREDRIK:
   My Anne.

DESIRÉE:
   Sorry — Anne.

FREDRIK:
   She loves my voice, my walk, my mustache,
   The cigar, in fact, that I'm smoking.
   She'll watch me puff until it's just ash,
   Then she'll save the cigar butt.

DESIRÉE:
   Bizarre, but
   You're joking.

FREDRIK:
   She dotes on —

DESIRÉE:
   Your dimple.

FREDRIK:
   My snoring.

DESIRÉE:
   How dear.

FREDRIK:
   The point is, she's really simple.

DESIRÉE (*Smiling*):
   Yes, that much seems clear.

FREDRIK:

She gives me funny names.

DESIRÉE:

Like — ?

FREDRIK:

"Old dry-as-dust."

DESIRÉE:

Wouldn't she just?

FREDRIK:

You must meet my wife.

DESIRÉE:

If I must —

> (*Looks over her shoulder at him and smiles*)

Yes, I must.

FREDRIK:

A sea of whims that I submerge in,
Yet so lovable in repentance.
Unfortunately, still a virgin,
But you can't force a flower —

DESIRÉE (*Rises*):

Don't finish that sentence!
She's monstrous!

FREDRIK:

She's frightened.

DESIRÉE:

Unfeeling!

FREDRIK:

Unversed.
She'd strike you as unenlightened.

DESIRÉE:

No, I'd strike her first.

FREDRIK:
  Her reticence, her apprehension —

DESIRÉE:
  Her crust!

FREDRIK:
  No!

DESIRÉE:
  Yes!

FREDRIK:
  No!

DESIRÉE:
  Fredrik . . .

FREDRIK:
  You must meet my wife.

DESIRÉE:
  Let me get my hat and my knife.

FREDRIK:
  What was that?

DESIRÉE:
  I must meet your wife.

FREDRIK: DESIRÉE:
Yes, you must.   Yes, I must.

DESIRÉE (*Speaks*): A virgin.

FREDRIK: A virgin.

DESIRÉE: Eleven months?

FREDRIK: Eleven months.

DESIRÉE: No wonder you dreamed of me!

FREDRIK: At least it was you I dreamed of, which indicates a
  kind of retroactive fidelity, doesn't it?

DESIRÉE: At least.

FREDRIK (*Suddenly very shy*): Desirée, I —

DESIRÉE: Yes?

FREDRIK: Would it seem insensitive if I were to ask you — I can't say it!

DESIRÉE: Say it, darling.

FREDRIK: Would you . . .

(*He can't*)

DESIRÉE: Of course. What are old friends for?
(*She rises, holds out her hand to him. He takes her hand, rises, too*)
Wait till you see the bedroom! Stockings all over the place, a rather rusty hip-bath — and the Virgin Mary over the headboard.
(*They exit, laughing, into the bedroom.* MADAME ARM-FELDT *appears and sings, with one eye on the room*)

MADAME ARMFELDT:
At the villa of the Baron de Signac,
Where I spent a somewhat infamous year,
At the villa of the Baron de Signac
I had ladies in attendance,
Fire-opal pendants . . .

Liaisons! What's happened to them,
Liaisons today?
Disgraceful! What's become of them?
Some of them
Hardly pay their shoddy way.

What once was a rare champagne
Is now just an amiable hock,
What once was a villa at least
Is "digs."

66

What once was a gown with train
Is now just a simple little frock,
What once was a sumptuous feast
Is figs.
No, not even figs — raisins.
Ah, liaisons!

Now let me see . . . Where was I? Oh, yes . . .

At the palace of the Duke of Ferrara,
Who was prematurely deaf but a dear,
At the palace of the Duke of Ferrara
I acquired some position
Plus a tiny Titian . . .

Liaisons! What's happened to them,
Liaisons today?
To see them — indiscriminate
Women, it
Pains me more than I can say,
The lack of taste that they display.

Where is style?
Where is skill?
Where is forethought?
Where's discretion of the heart,
Where's passion in the art,
Where's craft?
With a smile
And a will,
But with more thought,
I acquired a chateau
Extravagantly o-
Verstaffed.

Too many people muddle sex
With mere desire,
And when emotion intervenes,

67

The nets descend.
It should on no account perplex,
Or worse, inspire.
It's but a pleasurable means
To a measurable end.
Why does no one comprehend?
Let us hope this lunacy is just a trend.

Now let me see . . . Where was I? Oh, yes . . .

In the castle of the King of the Belgians
We would visit through a false chiffonier.
In the castle of the King of the Belgians
Who, when things got rather touchy,
Deeded me a duchy . . .

Liaisons! What's happened to them,
Liaisons today?
Untidy — take my daughter, I
Taught her, I
Tried my best to point the way.
I even named her Desirée.

In a world where the kings are employers,
Where the amateur prevails and delicacy fails to pay,
In a world where the princes are lawyers,
What can anyone expect except to recollect
Liai . . .
  (*She falls asleep.* FRID *appears and carries her off. A beat*)

CARL-MAGNUS (*Off*): All right, all right. It's broken down. So *do* something! Crank it up — or whatever it is!
  (FREDRIK *and* DESIRÉE *appear at the bedroom door,* FREDRIK *in a bathrobe,* DESIRÉE *in a negligee*)

FREDRIK: What can it be?

DESIRÉE: It can't!

FREDRIK: The dragoon?

DESIRÉE: Impossible. He's on maneuvers. Eighty miles away. He couldn't . . .

CARL-MAGNUS (*Off, bellowing*): A garage, idiot! That's what they're called.

DESIRÉE: He could.

FREDRIK: Is he jealous?

DESIRÉE: Tremendously.
(*Suppresses a giggle*)
This shouldn't be funny, should it?

FREDRIK: Let him in.

DESIRÉE: Fredrik . . .

FREDRIK: I am not a lawyer — nor are you an actress — for nothing. Let him in.
(DESIRÉE *goes to open the door.* CARL-MAGNUS *enters, immaculate but brushing imaginary dust from his uniform. He is carrying a bunch of daisies*)

DESIRÉE (*With tremendous poise*): Carl-Magnus! What a delightful surprise!
(*Totally ignoring* FREDRIK, CARL-MAGNUS *bows stiffly and kisses her hand*)

CARL-MAGNUS: Excuse my appearance. My new motorcar broke down.
(*Hand kiss. Presents the daisies*)
From a neighboring garden.

DESIRÉE (*Taking them*): How lovely! Will you be staying long?

CARL-MAGNUS: I have twenty hours leave. Three hours coming here, nine hours with you, five hours with my wife and three hours back.
(*Still ignoring* FREDRIK)
Do you mind if I take off my uniform and put on my robe?

69

DESIRÉE: Well — at the moment it's occupied.

CARL-MAGNUS (*Not looking at* FREDRIK): So I see.

DESIRÉE: Mr. Egerman — Count Malcolm.

FREDRIK: Sir.

CARL-MAGNUS (*Still ignoring* FREDRIK): Sir.

FREDRIK: I feel I should give you an explanation for what may seem to be a rather unusual situation.
(*With tremulous aplomb*)
For many years, I have been Miss Armfeldt's mother's lawyer and devoted friend. A small lawsuit of hers — nothing major, I'm happy to say — comes up in Court tomorrow morning and at the last minute I realized that some legal papers required her daughter's signature. Although it was late and she had already retired . . .

DESIRÉE: I let him in, of course.

CARL-MAGNUS (*Turning the icy gaze on her*): And then?

DESIRÉE: Ah, yes, the — the robe. Well, you see . . .

FREDRIK: Unfortunately, sir, on my way to the water-closet — through Miss Armfeldt's darkened bedroom — I inadvertently tripped over her hip-bath and fell in. Miss Armfeldt generously loaned me this garment while waiting for my clothes to dry in the bedroom.

CARL-MAGNUS: In that case, Miss Armfeldt, I suggest you return to the bedroom and see whether this gentleman's clothes are dry by now.

DESIRÉE: Yes. Of course.
(*She crosses between* FREDRIK *and* CARL-MAGNUS *and exits. Pacing,* CARL-MAGNUS *begins to whistle a military march.* FREDRIK *counters by whistling a bit of Mozart*)

CARL-MAGNUS: Are you fond of duels, sir?

FREDRIK: I don't really know. I haven't ever tried.

CARL-MAGNUS: I have duelled seven times. Pistol, rapier, foil. I've been wounded five times. Otherwise fortune has been kind to me.

FREDRIK: I must say I'm impressed.

CARL-MAGNUS (*Picking up fruit knife*): You see this fruit knife? The target will be that picture. The old lady. Her face. Her eye.
> (*Throws knife, which hits target*)

FREDRIK (*Clapping*): Bravo.

CARL-MAGNUS: Are you being insolent, sir?

FREDRIK: Of course — sir.
> (DESIRÉE *returns from the bedroom. She is carrying* FREDRIK's *clothes in a soaking wet bundle. She has dipped them in the hip-bath*)

DESIRÉE: They're not *very* dry.

FREDRIK: Oh dear me, they're certainly not, are they?

CARL-MAGNUS: A predicament.

FREDRIK: Indeed.

CARL-MAGNUS: I imagine, Miss Armfeldt, you could find this gentleman one of my nightshirts.

FREDRIK: Thank you, thank you. But I think I'd prefer to put on my own — er — garments.
> (FREDRIK *takes the wet bundle from* DESIRÉE)

CARL-MAGNUS: Unfortunately, sir, you will not have the time for that.
> (*To* DESIRÉE)
Perhaps you could tell him where to look.

DESIRÉE: Oh yes, yes. The left hand — no, the right hand

bottom drawer of the — er —
>*(Indicating a chest of drawers)*

. . . thing.

>(FREDRIK *gives her the wet clothes*)

FREDRIK (*Hesitating, then*): Thank you.
>(*He goes into the bedroom. While he is away,* DESIRÉE *and* CARL-MAGNUS *confront each other in near-silence:* CARL-MAGNUS *whistles a bit of the march that he whistled at* FREDRIK *earlier.* FREDRIK *returns in a nightshirt, carrying the robe, which he holds out to* CARL-MAGNUS)

Your robe, sir.
>(CARL-MAGNUS *receives it in silence.* FREDRIK *puts on the nightcap that goes with the nightshirt*)

Well — er — goodnight. Miss Armfeldt, thank you for your cooperation.
>(FREDRIK *takes the wet bundle from* DESIRÉE *and exits*)

CARL-MAGNUS (*Sings, to himself*):
She wouldn't . . .
Therefore they didn't . . .
So then it wasn't . . .
Not unless it . . .
Would she?
She doesn't . . .
God knows she needn't . . .
Therefore it's not.

He'd never . . .
Therefore they haven't . . .
Which makes the question absolutely . . .
Could he?
She daren't . . .
Therefore I mustn't . . .
What utter rot!

Fidelity is more than mere display,

It's what a man expects from life.

(*The unit that* DESIRÉE *is sitting on starts to ride off as* CHARLOTTE, *seated at her breakfast table, rides on*)

Fidelity like mine to Desirée
And Charlotte, my devoted wife.

Scene 5

BREAKFAST ROOM IN MALCOLM COUNTRY HOUSE

Breakfast for one (CHARLOTTE's) — *and an extra coffee cup* — *stands on an elegant little table. Music under.*

CHARLOTTE: How was Miss Desirée Armfeldt? In good health, I trust?

CARL-MAGNUS: Charlotte, my dear. I have exactly five hours.

CHARLOTTE (*Dead pan*): Five hours this time? Last time it was four. I'm gaining ground.

CARL-MAGNUS (*Pre-occupied*): She had a visitor. A lawyer in a nightshirt.

CHARLOTTE: Now, *that* I find interesting. What did you do?

CARL-MAGNUS: Threw him out.

CHARLOTTE: In a nightshirt?

CARL-MAGNUS: In *my* nightshirt.

CHARLOTTE: What sort of lawyer? Corporation, maritime, criminal — testamentary?

CARL-MAGNUS: Didn't your sister's little school friend Anne Sorensen marry a Fredrik Egerman?

CHARLOTTE: Yes, she did.

CARL-MAGNUS: Fredrik Egerman . . .
                              (*Sings*)

> The papers,
> He mentioned papers,
> Some legal papers
> Which I didn't see there . . .
> Where were they,
> The goddamn papers
> She had to sign?

> What nonsense!
> He brought her papers,
> They were important,
> So he had to be there . . .
> I'll kill him . . .
> Why should I bother?
> The woman's mine!

> Besides, no matter what one might infer,
> One must have faith to some degree.
> The least that I can do is trust in her
> The way that Charlotte trusts in me.
>   (*Speaks*)
> What are you planning to do today?

CHARLOTTE: *After* the five hours?

CARL-MAGNUS: Right now. I need a little sleep.

CHARLOTTE: Ah! I see. In that case, my plans will have to be changed. What will I do?
                              (*Sudden mock radiance*)
I know! Nothing!

CARL-MAGNUS: Why don't you pay a visit to Marta's little school friend?

CHARLOTTE: Ah ha!

CARL-MAGNUS: She probably has no idea what *her* husband's up to.

CHARLOTTE: And I could enlighten her. Poor Carl-Magnus, are you *that* jealous?

CARL-MAGNUS: A civilized man can tolerate his wife's infidelity, but when it comes to his mistress, a man becomes a tiger.

CHARLOTTE: As opposed, of course, to a goat in rut. Ah, well, if I'm back in two hours, that still leaves us three hours. Right?

CARL-MAGNUS (*Unexpectedly smiling*): You're a good wife, Charlotte. The best.

CHARLOTTE: That's a comforting thought to take with me to town, dear. It just may keep me from cutting my throat on the tram.

(CHARLOTTE *exits*)

CARL-MAGNUS:
Capable, pliable . . .
Women, women . . .
Undemanding and reliable,
Knowing their place.
Insufferable, yes, but gentle,
Their weaknesses are incidental,
A functional but ornamental
                    (*Sips coffee*)
Race.
Durable, sensible . . .
Women, women . . .
Very nearly indispensable
Creatures of grace.
God knows the foolishness about them,

But if one had to live without them,
The world would surely be a poorer,
If purer,
Place.

The hip-bath . . .
About that hip-bath . . .
How can you slip and trip into a hip-bath?
The papers . . .
Where were the papers?
Of course, he might have taken back the papers . . .
She wouldn't . . .
Therefore they didn't . . .
The woman's mine!
                    (*He strides off*)

Scene 6

THE EGERMAN ROOMS

In the bedroom, ANNE, *in a negligee, sits on the bed while* PETRA *combs her hair.*

ANNE: Oh, that's delicious. I could purr. Having your hair brushed is gloriously sensual, isn't it?

PETRA: I can think of more sensual things.

ANNE (*Giggles, then suddenly serious*): Are you a virgin, Petra?

PETRA: God forbid.

ANNE (*Sudden impulse*): I am.

PETRA: I know.

ANNE (*Astonished and flustered*): How on earth can you tell?

PETRA: Your skin, something in your eyes.

ANNE: Can everyone see it?

PETRA: I wouldn't think so.

ANNE: Well, that's a relief.

(*Giggles*)

How old were you when —

PETRA: Sixteen.

ANNE: It must have been terrifying, wasn't it? *And* disgusting.

PETRA: Disgusting? It was more fun than the rolly-coaster at the fair.

ANNE: Henrik says that almost everything that's fun is automatically vicious. It's so depressing.

PETRA: Oh him! Poor little puppy dog!

ANNE (*Suddenly imperious*): Don't you dare talk about your employer's son that way.

PETRA: Sorry, Ma'am.

ANNE: I forbid anyone in this house to tease Henrik.
(*Giggles again*)
Except me.
(ANNE *goes to the vanity, sits, opens the top of her robe, studies her reflection in the table-mirror*)
It's quite a good body, isn't it?

PETRA: Nothing wrong there.

ANNE: Is it as good as yours?
(*Laughing, she turns and pulls at* PETRA, *trying to undo* PETRA*'s uniform*)
Let me see!
(*For a moment,* PETRA *is shocked. Laughing,* ANNE *continues;* PETRA *starts laughing too. They begin struggling playfully together*)
If I was a boy, would I prefer you or me? Tell me, tell me!
(*Still laughing and struggling they stumble across the room and collapse in a heap on the bed*)
You're a boy! You're a boy!

PETRA (*Laughing*): God forbid!

79

(As they struggle, the front doorbell rings)

ANNE *(Sits up)*: Run, Petra, run. Answer it.
>*(PETRA climbs over ANNE to get off of the bed. As PETRA hurries into the parlor and exits to answer the door, ANNE peers at herself in the mirror)*

Oh dear, oh dear, my hair! My — everything!
>*(PETRA returns to the parlor with CHARLOTTE)*

PETRA: Please have a seat, Countess. Madame will be with you in a minute.
>*(CHARLOTTE looks around the room — particularly at FREDRIK's picture. PETRA hurries into the bedroom. Hissing)*

It's a Countess!

ANNE: A Countess?

PETRA: Very grand.

ANNE: How thrilling! Who on earth can she be?
>*(After a final touch at the mirror, she draws herself up with great dignity and, with PETRA behind her, sweeps into the parlor. At the door, she stops and stares. Then delighted, runs to CHARLOTTE)*

Charlotte Olafsson! It is, isn't it? Marta's big sister who married that magnificent Count Something or Other — and I was a flower girl at the wedding.

CHARLOTTE: Unhappily without a time-bomb in your Lilly-of-the-Valley bouquet.

ANNE *(Laughing)*: Oh, Charlotte, you always did say the most amusing things.

CHARLOTTE: I still do. I frequently laugh myself to sleep contemplating my own future.

ANNE: Petra. Ice, lemonade, cookies.
>*(PETRA leaves. Pause)*

CHARLOTTE: Well, dear, how are you? And how is your marriage working out?

ANNE: I'm in bliss. I have all the dresses in the world and a maid to take care of me and this charming house and a husband who spoils me shamelessly.

CHARLOTTE: That list, I trust, is in diminishing order of priority.

ANNE: How dreadful you are! Of course it isn't. And how's dear Marta?

CHARLOTTE: Ecstatic. Dear Marta has renounced men and is teaching gymnastics in a school for retarded girls in Bettleheim. Which brings me or . . .
(*Glancing at a little watch on her bosom*)
. . . rather should bring me, as my time is strictly limited — to the subject of men. How do you rate your husband as a man?

ANNE: I — don't quite know what you mean.

CHARLOTTE: I will give you an example. As a man, my husband could be rated as a louse, a bastard, a conceited, puffed-up, adulterous egomaniac. He constantly makes me do the most degrading, the most humiliating things like . . . like . . .
(*Her composure starts to crumble. She opens a little pocketbook and fumbles*)

ANNE: Like?

CHARLOTTE: Like . . .
(*Taking tiny handkerchief from purse, dabbing at her nose and bursting into tears*)
Oh, why do I put up with it? Why do I let him treat me like — like an intimidated corporal in his regiment? Why? Why? Why? I'll tell you why. I despise him! I hate

him! I *love* him! Oh damn that woman! May she rot forever in some infernal dressing room with lipstick of fire and scalding mascara! Let every billboard in hell eternally announce: Desirée Armfeldt in — in — in *The Wild Duck!*
(*Abandons herself to tears*)

ANNE: Desirée Armfeldt? But what has she done to you?

CHARLOTTE: What has she *not* done? Enslaved my husband — enslaved yours . . .

ANNE: Fredrik!

CHARLOTTE: He was there last night in her bedroom — in a nightshirt. My husband threw him out into the street and he's insanely jealous. He told me to come here and tell you . . . and I'm actually *telling* you! Oh what a monster I've become!

ANNE: Charlotte, is that the truth? Fredrik was there — in a nightshirt?
(CHARLOTTE *sobs*)

CHARLOTTE: My husband's nightshirt!

ANNE: Oh I knew it! I was sure he'd met her before. And when she *smiled* at us in the theater . . .
(*She begins to weep*)

CHARLOTTE: Poor Anne!
(PETRA *enters with the tray of lemonade and cookies and stands gazing at the two women in astonishment*)

PETRA: The lemonade, Ma'am.

ANNE: (*Looking up, controlling herself with a great effort, to the weeping* CHARLOTTE): Lemonade, Charlotte?

CHARLOTTE (*Looking up too, seeing the lemonade*): Lemonade! It would choke me!
(*Sings*)

82

Every day a little death
In the parlor, in the bed,
In the curtains, in the silver,
In the buttons, in the bread.
Every day a little sting
In the heart and in the head.
Every move and every breath,
And you hardly feel a thing,
Brings a perfect little death.

He smiles sweetly, strokes my hair,
Says he misses me.
I would murder him right there,
But first I die.
He talks softly of his wars,
And his horses
And his whores,
I think love's a dirty business!

ANNE: So do I!

CHARLOTTE: ANNE:
I'm before him   So do I . . .
On my knees
And he kisses me.

CHARLOTTE:
He assumes I'll lose my reason,
And I do.
Men are stupid, men are vain,
Love's disgusting, love's insane,
A humiliating business!

ANNE:
Oh, how true!

CHARLOTTE:
Ah, well . . .
Every day a little death,

ANNE:

Every day a little death,

CHARLOTTE:

In the parlor, in the bed,

ANNE:

On the lips and in the eyes,

CHARLOTTE:

In the curtains,
In the silver,
In the buttons,
In the bread.

Every day a little sting
In the heart
And in the head.

ANNE:

In the murmurs,
In the pauses,
In the gestures,
In the sighs.

Every day a little dies,

In the looks and in
The lies.

Every move and
Every breath,
And you hardly feel a
Thing,
Brings a perfect little
Death.

And you hardly feel a
Thing,
Brings a perfect little
Death.

> (*After the number,* HENRIK *enters, taking off his hat and scarf*)

HENRIK: Oh, excuse me.

ANNE (*Trying to rise to the occasion*): Charlotte, this is Henrik Egerman.

HENRIK (*Bows and offers his hand*): I am happy to make your acquaintance, Madame.

CHARLOTTE: Happy! Who could ever be happy to meet *me?*

(*Holding* HENRIK'*s hand, she rises and then drifts out.* ANNE *falls back sobbing on the couch.* HENRIK *stands, gazing at her*)

HENRIK: Anne, what is it?

ANNE: Nothing.

HENRIK: But what did that woman say to you?

ANNE: Nothing, nothing at all.

HENRIK: That can't be true.

ANNE: It is! It is! She — she merely told me that Marta Olafsson, my dearest friend from school is — teaching gymnastics . . .
(*Bursts into tears again, falls into* HENRIK'*s arms.* HENRIK *puts his arms around her slowly, cautiously*)

HENRIK: Anne! Poor Anne! If you knew how it destroys me to see you unhappy.

ANNE: I am not unhappy!

HENRIK: You know. You must know. Ever since you married Father, you've been more precious to me than . . .

ANNE (*Pulls back, suddenly giggling through her tears*): . . . Martin Luther?
(HENRIK, *cut to the quick, jumps up*)

HENRIK: Can you laugh at me even now?

ANNE (*Rises*): Oh dear, I'm sorry. Perhaps, after all, I am a totally frivolous woman with ice for a heart. Am I, Henrik? *Am I?*
(PETRA *enters*)

MADAME ARMFELDT (*Off*): Seven of Hearts on the Eight of Spades.

ANNE (*Laughing again*): Silly Henrik, get your book, quick,

85

and denounce the wickedness of the world to me for at least a half an hour.

(ANNE *runs off as the bedroom and parlor go.* HENRIK *follows her, as does* PETRA, *carrying the lemonade tray*)

MADAME ARMFELDT (*Off*): The Ten of Hearts! Who needs the Ten of Hearts!!

Scene 7

ARMFELDT TERRACE

> MADAME ARMFELDT *is playing solitaire, with* FRID *standing behind her.* FREDRIKA *sits at the piano, playing scales.*

MADAME ARMFELDT: Child, I am about to give you your advice for the day.

FREDRIKA: Yes, Grandmother.

MADAME ARMFELDT: Never marry — or even dally with — a Scandinavian.

FREDRIKA: Why not, Grandmother?

MADAME ARMFELDT: They are all insane.

FREDRIKA: All of them?

MADAME ARMFELDT: Uh-hum. It's the latitude. A winter when the sun never rises, a summer when the sun never sets, are more than enough to addle the brain of any man. Further off, further off. You practically inhaled the Queen of Diamonds.

DESIRÉE (*Off*): Who's home?

FREDRIKA (*Jumps up, thrilled*): Mother!

(DESIRÉE *enters and* FREDRIKA *rushes to her, throwing herself into* DESIRÉE*'s arms*)

DESIRÉE: Darling, you've grown a mile; you're much prettier, you're irresistible! Hello, Mother.

MADAME ARMFELDT (*Continuing to play, unfriendly*): And to what do I owe the honor of this visit?

DESIRÉE: I just thought I'd pop out and see you both. Is that so surprising?

MADAME ARMFELDT: Yes.

DESIRÉE: You're in one of your bitchy moods, I see.

MADAME ARMFELDT: If you've come to take Fredrika back, the answer is no. I do not object to the immorality of your life, merely to its sloppiness. Since I have been tidy enough to have acquired a sizeable mansion with a fleet of servants, it is only common sense that my granddaughter should reap the advantages of it.
(*To* FREDRIKA)
Isn't that so, child?

FREDRIKA: I really don't know, Grandmother.

MADAME ARMFELDT: Oh yes you do, dear. Well, Desirée, there must be something you want or you wouldn't have "popped out." What is it?

DESIRÉE: All right. The tour's over for a while, and I was wondering if you'd invite some people here next weekend.

MADAME ARMFELDT: If they're actors, they'll have to sleep in the stables.

DESIRÉE: Not actors, Mother. Just a lawyer from town and his family — Fredrik Egerman.

88

MADAME ARMFELDT: In my day, one went to lawyers' offices but never consorted with their *families*.

DESIRÉE: Then it'll make a nice change, dear, won't it?

MADAME ARMFELDT: I am deeply suspicious, but very well.

DESIRÉE (*Producing a piece of paper*): Here's the address.

MADAME ARMFELDT (*Taking it*): I shall send 'round a formal invitation by hand.

> (*She snaps her fingers for* FRID. *As he wheels her off*)

Needless to say, I shall be polite to your guests. However, they will not be served my best champagne. I am saving that for my funeral.

> (FREDRIKA *runs to* DESIRÉE; *they embrace, and freeze in that pose. We see, in another area,* PETRA *bringing* ANNE *an invitation on a small silver tray*)

PETRA:
Look, Ma'am,
An invitation.
Here, Ma'am,
Delivered by hand.
And, Ma'am,
I notice the station-
Ery's engraved and very grand.

ANNE:
Petra, how too exciting!
Just when I need it!
Petra, such elegant writing,
So chic you hardly can read it.
What do you think?
Who can it be?
Even the ink —
No, here, let me . . .
"Your presence . . . "

89

Just think of it, Petra!
"Is kindly . . . "
It's at a chateau!
"Requested . . . "
Et cet'ra, et cet'ra,
". . . Madame Leonora Armf — "
Oh, no!
A weekend in the country!

PETRA:
We're invited?

ANNE:
What a horrible plot!
A weekend in the country!

PETRA:
I'm excited.

ANNE:
No, you're not!

PETRA:
A weekend in the country!
Just imagine!

ANNE:
It's completely depraved.

PETRA:
A weekend in the country!

ANNE:
It's insulting!

PETRA:
It's engraved.

ANNE:
It's that woman,
It's that Armfeldt . . .

PETRA:
Oh, the actress . . .

ANNE:
No, the ghoul.
She may hope to
Make her charm felt,
But she's mad if she thinks
I would be such a fool
As to weekend in the country!

PETRA (*Ironically*):
How insulting!

ANNE:
And I've nothing to wear!

BOTH:
A weekend in the country!

ANNE:
Here!
>   (ANNE *gives the invitation back to* PETRA)
The last place I'm going is there!
>   (ANNE *and* PETRA *exit.* DESIRÉE *and* FREDRIKA *unfreeze and begin to move downstage*)

DESIRÉE: Well, dear, are you happy here?

FREDRIKA: Yes. I think so. But I miss us.

DESIRÉE: Oh, so do I!
>   (*Pause*)
Darling, how would you feel if we had a home of our very own with me only acting when I felt like it — and a man who would make you a spectacular father?

FREDRIKA: Oh I see. The lawyer! Mr. Egerman!

DESIRÉE: Dear child, you're uncanny.

(DESIRÉE *and* FREDRIKA *freeze once again.* FREDRIK, ANNE, *and* PETRA *enter*)

PETRA (*To* FREDRIK):
Guess what, an invitation!

ANNE:
Guess who, begins with an "A" . . .
Armfeldt —
Is that a relation
To the decrepit Desirée?

PETRA:
Guess when we're asked to go, sir —
See, sir, the date there?
Guess where — a fancy chateau, sir!

ANNE:
Guess, too, who's lying in wait there,
Setting her traps,
Fixing her face —

FREDRIK:
Darling,
Perhaps a change of pace . . .

ANNE:	FREDRIK:
Oh, no!	A weekend in the country
	Would be charming,
	And the air would be fresh.

ANNE:
A weekend
With that woman . . .

FREDRIK:
In the country . . .

ANNE:
In the flesh!

FREDRIK:
I've some business
With her mother.

PETRA:
See, it's business!

ANNE:
. . . Oh, no doubt!
But the business
With her mother
Would be hardly the business I'd worry about.

FREDRIK *and* PETRA:
Just a weekend in the country,

FREDRIK:
Smelling jasmine . . .

ANNE:
Watching little things grow.

FREDRIK *and* PETRA:
A weekend in the country . . .

ANNE:
Go!

FREDRIK:
My darling,
We'll simply say no.

ANNE:
Oh.
                    (*They exit.* FREDRIKA *and* DESIRÉE *unfreeze*)

FREDRIKA: Oh, Mother, I know it's none of my business, but
. . . that dragoon you wrote me about — with the mustache?

DESIRÉE: Oh, him! What I ever saw in him astounds me.

He's a tin soldier — arms, legs, brain — tin, tin, tin!
(*They freeze on the downstage bench.* ANNE *and* CHAR-
LOTTE *enter*)

ANNE:
A weekend!

CHARLOTTE:
How very amusing.

ANNE:
A weekend!

CHARLOTTE:
But also inept.

ANNE:
A weekend!
Of course, we're refusing.

CHARLOTTE:
Au contraire,
You must accept.

ANNE:
Oh, no!

CHARLOTTE:
A weekend in the country . . .

ANNE:
But it's frightful!

CHARLOTTE:
No, you don't understand.
A weekend in the country
Is delightful
If it's planned.
Wear your hair down
And a flower,
Don't use make-up,

Dress in white.
She'll grow older
By the hour
And be hopelessly shattered by
Saturday night.
Spend a weekend in the country.

ANNE:
We'll accept it!

CHARLOTTE:
I'd a feeling
You would.

BOTH:
A weekend in the country!

ANNE:
Yes, it's only polite that we should.

CHARLOTTE:
Good.
> (ANNE *and* CHARLOTTE *disappear.* DESIRÉE *and* FREDRIKA
> *unfreeze*)

FREDRIKA: Count Malcolm's insanely jealous, isn't he? You
don't suppose he'll come galloping up on a black stal-
lion, brandishing a sword?

DESIRÉE: Oh dear, I hadn't thought of that. But no, no,
thank heavens. It's his wife's birthday this weekend —
sacred to domesticity. At least we're safe from him.
> (*They freeze.* CARL-MAGNUS *enters;* CHARLOTTE *follows
> opposite to meet him*)

CARL-MAGNUS:
Well?

CHARLOTTE:
I've an intriguing little social item.

CARL-MAGNUS:
   What?

CHARLOTTE:
   Out at the Armfeldt family manse.

CARL-MAGNUS:
   Well, what?

CHARLOTTE:
   Merely a weekend,
   Still I thought it might am-
   Use you to know who's invited to go,
   This time with his pants.

CARL-MAGNUS:
   You don't mean — ?

CHARLOTTE:
   I'll give you three guesses.

CARL-MAGNUS:
   She wouldn't!

CHARLOTTE:
   Reduce it to two.

CARL-MAGNUS:
   It can't be . . .

CHARLOTTE:
   It nevertheless is . . .

CARL-MAGNUS:
   Egerman!

CHARLOTTE:
   Right! Score one for you.

CARL-MAGNUS (*Triumphantly*):
   Aha!

CHARLOTTE (*Triumphantly*):
   Aha!

CARL-MAGNUS (*Thoughtfully*):
   Aha!

CHARLOTTE (*Worriedly*):
   Aha?

CARL-MAGNUS:
   A weekend in the country . . .
   We should try it —

CHARLOTTE:
   How I wish we'd been asked.

CARL-MAGNUS:
   A weekend in the country . . .
   Peace and quiet —

CHARLOTTE:
   We'll go masked.

CARL-MAGNUS:
   A weekend in the country . . .

CHARLOTTE:
   Uninvited —
   They'll consider it odd.

CARL-MAGNUS:
   A weekend in the country —
   I'm delighted!

CHARLOTTE:
   Oh, my God.

CARL-MAGNUS:
   And the shooting should be pleasant
   If the weather's not too rough.
   Happy Birthday,
   It's your present.

97

CHARLOTTE:
   But —

CARL-MAGNUS:
   You haven't been getting out nearly enough,
   And a weekend in the country —

CHARLOTTE:
   It's perverted!

CARL-MAGNUS:
   Pack my quiver and bow.

BOTH:
   A weekend in the country —

CARL-MAGNUS:
   At exactly 2:30, we go.

CHARLOTTE:
   We can't.

CARL-MAGNUS:
   We shall.

CHARLOTTE:
   We shan't.

CARL-MAGNUS:
   I'm getting the car
   And we're motoring down.

CHARLOTTE:
   Yes, I'm certain you are
   And I'm staying in town.
            (ANNE, FREDRIK, *and* PETRA *appear*)

CARL-MAGNUS:	ANNE:
Go and pack my suits!	We'll go.
CHARLOTTE:	PETRA:
I won't!	Oh, good!

98

CARL-MAGNUS:
My boots!
Pack everything I own
That shoots.

CHARLOTTE:
No!

CARL-MAGNUS:
Charlotte!

CHARLOTTE:
I'm thinking it out.

CARL-MAGNUS:
Charlotte!

CHARLOTTE:
There's no need to shout.

CARL-MAGNUS:
Charlotte!

CHARLOTTE:
All right, then,

BOTH:
We're off on our way,

FREDRIK:
We will?

ANNE:
We should.
Pack everything white.

PETRA:
Ma'am, it's wonderful news!

FREDRIK:
Are you sure it's all right?

ANNE:
We'd be rude to refuse.

FREDRIK:
Then we're off!

PETRA:
We are?

FREDRIK:
We'll take the car.

ALL THREE:
We'll bring champagne
And caviar!
We're off on our way,

99

What a beautiful day   What a beautiful day
For   For

ALL:

> A weekend in the country,
> How amusing,
> How delightfully droll.
> A weekend in the country
> While we're losing our control.
> A weekend in the country,
> How enchanting
> On the manicured lawns.
> A weekend in the country,
> With the panting and the yawns.
> With the crickets and the pheasants
> And the orchards and the hay,
> With the servants and the peasants,
> We'll be laying our plans
> While we're playing croquet
> For a weekend in the country,
> So inactive that one has to lie down.
> A weekend in the country
> Where . . .

(HENRIK *enters*)

HENRIK:

> A weekend in the country,
> The bees in their hives,
> The shallow, worldly figures,
> The frivolous lives.
> The devil's companions
> Know not whom they serve.
> It might be instructive
> To observe.

(DESIRÉE *and* FREDRIKA *unfreeze*)

DESIRÉE: However, there is one tiny snag.

FREDRIKA: A snag?

DESIRÉE: Lawyer Egerman is married.

FREDRIKA: That could be considered a snag.

DESIRÉE: Don't worry, my darling. I was not raised by your Grandmother for nothing.

(DESIRÉE *holds out her arm, and* FREDRIKA *runs to her. Together, they walk upstage as we see, for the first time, the facade of the Armfeldt mansion.* FRID *stands at the door, and once* DESIRÉE *and* FREDRIKA *have entered, he closes it behind them*)

CARL-MAGNUS: Charlotte!	FREDRIK: We're off!	HENRIK: A weekend in the Country, The bees in their Hives . . .
CHARLOTTE: I'm thinking it out.	PETRA: We are?	
CARL-MAGNUS: Charlotte!	FREDRIK *and* ANNE: We'll take the car.	
CHARLOTTE: There's no need To shout.	ALL THREE: We'll bring Champagne and Caviar!	MRS. SEGSTROM *and* MRS. ANDERSSEN: We're off! We are? We'll take the car.

MRS. NORDSTROM
and MR. ERLANSON:
A weekend of
  playing
Croquet
A weekend of
  strolling
The lawns,
	MR. LINDQUIST:
	Confiding our
	  motives
	
	And hiding our
	  yawns,
		MRS. ANDERSSEN *and*
		MRS. SEGSTROM:
		We'll
		
		Bring
		Champagne
		
		And caviar!

101

CARL-MAGNUS, CHARLOTTE,
FREDRIK, ANNE, *and* PETRA:
We're off and away,
What a beautiful day!

QUINTET:
The weather is spectacular!

ALL:
   With riotous laughter
   We quietly suffer
   The season in town,
   Which is reason enough for
   A weekend in the country,
   How amusing,
   How delightfully droll!
   A weekend in the country,
   While we're losing our control.
   A weekend in the country,
   How enchanting
   On the manicured lawns.
   A weekend in the country,
   With the panting and the yawns.
   With the crickets and the pheasants
   And the orchards and the hay,
   With the servants and the peasants,
   We'll be laying our plans
   While we're playing croquet
   For a weekend in the country,
   So inactive that one has to lie down.
   A weekend in the country
   Where . . .
   We're twice as upset as in
   Twice as upset as in
   Twice as upset as in
   Twice as upset as in . . .
                (*All, simultaneously*)

QUINTET:
Twice as upset as in,

Twice as upset as in,
Twice as upset as in,
Twice as upset as in,
Twice as upset as in,
Twice as upset as in,
Twice as upset as in,
Twice as upset as in,
Twice as upset as in —

ANNE:
Twice as upset as in town.
A weekend!
A weekend!
A weekend!
A weekend!
A weekend!
A weekend out of —

FREDRIK:
Twice as upset . . .
Are you sure you want to go?
Are you sure you want to go?
Are you sure you want to go
Away and leave,
Go and leave — ?

CHARLOTTE:
Twice as upset . . .
We're uninvited,
Uninvited,
Uninvited —
We should stay in —

CARL-MAGNUS:
Twice as upset . . .
Charlotte, we're going,
Charlotte, we're going,
Charlotte, we're going,
Charlotte, out of —

PETRA:
Twice as upset . . .
A weekend!
A weekend!
A weekend!
A weekend!
A weekend!
A weekend!
A weekend out of —

HENRIK:
Shallow, worldly
People going,
Shallow people
Going out of —

ALL:
  Town!

(*Curtain*)

103

Glynis Johns as Desirée Armfeldt

"The Overture" as sung by the Quintet: Mr. Lindquist (Benjamin Rayson), Mrs. Nordstrom (Teri Ralston), Mr. Erlanson (Gene Varrone), Mrs. Segstrom (Beth Fowler) and Mrs. Anderssen (Barbara Lang)

VAN WILLIAMS

"Night Waltz"

VAN WILLIAMS

Victoria Mallory as Anne Egerman

Frid (George Lee Andrews), Fredrika Armfeldt (Judy Kahan) and Madame Armfeldt (Hermione Gingold)

"Later"
Henrik Egerman (Mark Lambert)

Len Cariou as Fredrik Egerman

"Now"
Fredrik (Len Cariou) and Anne (Victoria Mallory)

Mrs. Anderssen (Barbara Lang) and Mrs. Segstrom (Beth Fowler) in their roles as Madame Merville and Madame Vilmorac

Desirée (Glynis Johns)

"Liaisons"
Madame Armfeldt (Hermione Gingold)

"You Must Meet My Wife"
Fredrik (Len Cariou) and Desirée (Glynis Johns)

"In Praise of Women"
Count Carl-Magnus Malcolm (Laurence
Guittard) and Desirée (Glynis Johns)

"Every Day a Little Death"
Countess Charlotte Malcolm (Patricia
Elliott) and Anne (Victoria Mallory)

VAN WILLIAMS

"A Weekend in the Country"

The opening of Act II. Charlotte (Patricia Elliott), Fredrika (Judy Kahan), Carl-Magnus (Laurence Guittard), Desirée (Glynis Johns), Fredrik (Len Cariou) and Anne (Victoria Mallory)

VAN WILLIAMS

123

Frid (George Lee Andrews) and Petra (D. Jamin-Bartlett)

Desirée (Glynis Johns) and Fredrik (Len Cariou)

Sally Ann Howes as Desirée Armfeldt

Above, George Lee Andrews as Fredrik Egerman and Michael Maguire as Count Carl-Magnus Malcolm; *below*, Desirée Armfeldt (Sally Ann Howes), Madame Armfeldt (Regina Resnik) and servants

Regina Resnik as Madame Armfeldt

ZOE DOMINIC

Jean Simmons as Desirée Armfeldt

Fredrik Egerman (Joss Ackland), Desirée Armfeldt (Jean Simmons), Anne Egerman (Veronica Page), Madame Armfeldt (Hermione Gingold), Henrik Egerman (Terry Mitchell), Count Carl-Magnus Malcolm (David Kernan) and Countess Charlotte Malcolm (Maria Atiken)

The Motion Picture. Frederick Egerman (Len Cariou), Desirée Armfeldt (Elizabeth Taylor), Carl-Magnus Mittelheim (Laurence Guittard) and Charlotte Mittelheim (Diana Rigg)

ACT II

Entr'acte

After a musical entr'acte, the QUINTET *enters.*

MRS. ANDERSSEN:
The sun sits low,
Diffusing its usual glow.
Five o'clock . . .
Twilight . . .
Vespers sound,
And it's six o'clock . . .
Twilight
All around,

ALL:
But the sun sits low,
As low as it's going to go.

MR. ERLANSON:
Eight o'clock . . .

MR. LINDQUIST:
Twilight . . .

WOMEN:
How enthralling!

MR. ERLANSON:
It's nine o'clock . . .

MR. LINDQUIST:
Twilight . . .

WOMEN:
Slowly crawling
Towards

MR. ERLANSON:
Ten o'clock . . .

MR. LINDQUIST:
Twilight . . .

WOMEN:
Crickets calling,

ALL:
The vespers ring,
The nightingale's waiting to sing.
The rest of us wait on a string.
Perpetual sunset
Is rather an unset-
Tling thing.

(*The show curtain rises on Scene 1*)

Scene 1

THE ARMFELDT LAWN

> FRID *is serving champagne to* DESIRÉE *and* MALLA.
> FREDRIKA, *upstage, is playing croquet with the help of*
> BERTRAND, MADAME ARMFELDT'*s page.* FRID *returns to*
> MADAME ARMFELDT. OSA, MADAME ARMFELDT'*s maid,*
> *passes with a tray of cookies, and* FREDRIKA *takes one.*
> DESIRÉE *gets a mallet and begins to play croquet.*

MADAME ARMFELDT: To lose a lover or even a husband or two
during the course of one's life can be vexing. But to lose
one's teeth is a catastrophe. Bear that in mind, child, as
you chomp so recklessly into that ginger snap.

FREDRIKA: Very well, Grandmother.

MADAME ARMFELDT (*Holding up her glass to* FRID): More champagne, Frid.
> (FRID *gets a fresh bottle*)
One bottle the less of the Mumms '87 will not, I hope,
diminish the hilarity at my wake.
> (DESIRÉE *sits on the rise.* FRID *opens the bottle with a loud*
> *pop!*)

QUINTET:
The sun won't set.

135

It's useless to hope or to fret.
It's dark as it's going to get.
The hands on the clock turn,
But don't sing a nocturne
Just yet.

(*Off, we hear a car-horn*)

DESIRÉE: They're coming!

MADAME ARMFELDT: Nonsense!

DESIRÉE: But they are!

MADAME ARMFELDT: Impossible. No guest with the slightest grasp of what is seemly would arrive before five-fifteen on a Friday afternoon.
    (*We hear the car-horn again, and this time it's louder*)
Good God, you're right!

DESIRÉE: Malla!

    (DESIRÉE *runs up into the house, followed closely by* MALLA *and* OSA. BERTRAND *exits with the croquet set*)

MADAME ARMFELDT: Frid! We cannot be caught squatting on the ground like Bohemians!

    (FRID *scoops her up and carries her into the house.* FREDRIKA *follows. The* QUINTET *runs on to collect the furniture and props left on stage. They freeze for a moment at the sound of the car-horn, and then all run off. A beat later,* CARL-MAGNUS'*s sports car drives on.* CARL-MAGNUS *is driving;* CHARLOTTE *sits beside him.* CARL-MAGNUS *stops the car and gets out*)

CHARLOTTE (*Looking around*): Happy birthday to me!

CARL-MAGNUS (*Inspecting a wheel*): What was that?

CHARLOTTE: I merely said . . . oh, never mind.

CARL-MAGNUS: If that damn lawyer thinks he's going to get away with something — Haha!

136

CHARLOTTE: Haha! indeed, dear.

>   (CARL-MAGNUS *helps* CHARLOTTE *out of the car*)

CARL-MAGNUS: Watch him, Charlotte. Watch them both like
a . . .

CHARLOTTE: Hawk. I know, dear. You're a tiger, I'm a hawk.
We're our own zoo.

>   (*As she speaks, a touring car sweeps on from the opposite
>   side. It is driven rather erratically by* FREDRIK *with* ANNE
>   *beside him.* HENRIK *and* PETRA *are in the back seat with a
>   pile of luggage. The car only just misses* CARL-MAGNUS'*s
>   car as it shudders to a stop. Recognition comes.* FREDRIK
>   *gets out of his car*)

FREDRIK: Good day, sir. I was not aware that you were to be a
fellow guest.

>   (FREDRIK *opens the car door and helps* ANNE *out.* HENRIK
>   *helps* PETRA *out of the back seat*)

CARL-MAGNUS: Neither is Miss Armfeldt. I hope our arrival
will in no way inconvenience you.

FREDRIK: Not at all, not at all. I am happy to see that you
have gotten through yet another week without any serious wounds.

CARL-MAGNUS: What's that? Wounds, sir?

FREDRIK: Rapier? Bow and arrow? Blow dart?

>   (*At this point,* ANNE *and* CHARLOTTE *see each other. They
>   run together. On the way,* ANNE *drops her handkerchief*)

ANNE (*Hissing*):	CHARLOTTE (*Hissing*):
So you did come?	So you did come?
(*Pause*)	(*Pause*)
Talk later.	Talk later.

>   (HENRIK, *tremendously solicitous, holds out the handker-
>   chief to* ANNE)

HENRIK: Your handkerchief, Anne.

ANNE (*Taking it, moving away*): Thank you.

HENRIK: You must have dropped it.
>   (PETRA *taps* HENRIK *on the shoulder*)

PETRA: Your book, Master Henrik.

HENRIK (*Taking it*): Thank you.

PETRA (*With soupy mock-solicitousness*): You must have dropped it.
>   (PETRA *moves to get the luggage.* FRID, *seeing and immediately appreciating* PETRA, *goes to her*)

FRID: Here. Let me.

PETRA (*Handing him two suitcases*): Let you — what?
>   (PETRA, *with one suitcase, enters the house, followed by* FRID, *who is carrying two.* HENRIK *is moodily drifting away as* DESIRÉE *emerges from the house. She is followed by* FREDRIKA, *and smiling dazzlingly for the* EGERMANS)

DESIRÉE: Ah, here you all are . . .
>   (CARL-MAGNUS *clears his throat noisily. The smile dies*)
> Count Malcolm!

CARL-MAGNUS (*Bowing frigidly over her hand*): My wife and I were in the neighborhood to visit her cousin. Unhappily, on arrival, we discovered the chateau was quarantined for . . .
>   (*Snaps his fingers at* CHARLOTTE)

CHARLOTTE: Plague.

CARL-MAGNUS: Since I am due back to maneuvers by dawn, we venture to propose ourselves for the night.

DESIRÉE (*Concealing no little fluster*): Well, yes. Indeed. Why not? Mother will be honored! — surprised, but honored.
>   (DESIRÉE *crosses to* CHARLOTTE, *and sweeps past her, barely touching her hand*)
> Countess Malcolm, I presume?

138

CHARLOTTE (*As* DESIRÉE *sweeps past her*): You do indeed, Miss Armfeldt.

DESIRÉE: And Mr. Egerman! How kind of you all to come. Mother will be overjoyed.

FREDRIK (*Bending over her hand*): It is your mother who is kind in inviting us. Allow me to present my rather anti-social son, Henrik.
(*Points to the drifting away* HENRIK, *who turns to acknowledge her*)
And this is my wife.
(*He presents* ANNE)

DESIRÉE: How do you do?

ANNE (*Icy*): How do you do?

DESIRÉE (*Indicating* FREDRIKA): And this is *my* daughter.
(*Pause*)
You must all be exhausted after your journeys; my daughter will show you to your rooms. Mother likes dinner at nine.
(FREDRIKA *leads them into the house:* CHARLOTTE, *then* ANNE, *then* HENRIK, *then* OSA. FREDRIKA *returns to the terrace. Simultaneously, both* FREDRIK *and* CARL-MAGNUS *turn, both with the same idea: to get* DESIRÉE *alone*)

CARL-MAGNUS *and* FREDRIK: Where shall I put the car?
(*They exchange a hostile glare*)

DESIRÉE (*Even more flustered*): Ah, the cars, the cars! Now let me see.

CARL-MAGNUS (*Hissing*): I must speak to you at once!

DESIRÉE (*Whispering*): Later.
(*Out loud*)
How about the stables? They're straight ahead.

FREDRIK (*Hissing*): I must speak to you at once!

139

DESIRÉE (*Whispering*): Later.

> (*Reassured,* CARL-MAGNUS *and* FREDRIK *return to their cars. Calling after him*)

You can't miss them, Mr. Egerman. Just look for the weather vane. A huge tin cockerel.

> (*Spinning to* FREDRIKA, *pulling her downstage*)

Disaster, darling!

FREDRIKA: But what are you going to do? The way he glared at Mr. Egerman! He'll kill him!

DESIRÉE: Let us keep calm.

> (FREDRIK *and* CARL-MAGNUS, *both with auto-cranks in hand, start back toward* DESIRÉE)

FREDRIKA (*Noticing*): They're coming back!

DESIRÉE (*Totally losing her calm*): Oh no! Oh God!

> (DESIRÉE *starts to run up to the house*)

FREDRIKA (*Calling after her*): But what should I say?

DESIRÉE: Anything!

> (*She runs into the house, as* FREDRIK *and* CARL-MAGNUS, *gazing after* DESIRÉE *in astonishment, come up to* FREDRIKA)

FREDRIKA (*On the spot but gracious, seemingly composed*): Mr. Egerman — Count Malcolm . . . Mother told me to tell you that she suddenly . . .

> (*She breaks*)

. . . oh dear, oh dear.

> (*She scurries up into the house. The two men react, then, ignoring each other, return to their cars. They each crank their cars and get into them. The cars back out offstage.* MR. ERLANSON *and* MRS. NORDSTROM *enter*)

MRS. NORDSTROM:

The sun sits low
And the vespers ring,

140

MR. ERLANSON:
   And the shadows grow
   And the crickets sing,
   And it's . . .

MRS. NORDSTROM:
   Look! Is that the moon?

MR. ERLANSON:
   Yes.
   What a lovely afternoon!

MRS. NORDSTROM:
   Yes.

MR. ERLANSON:
   The evening air
   Doesn't feel quite right

MRS. NORDSTROM:
   In the not-quite glare
   Of the not-quite night,
   And it's . . .
   Wait! Is that a star?

MR. ERLANSON:
   No.
   Just the glow of a cigar.

MRS. NORDSTROM:
   Oh.
                                        (*They exit*)

Scene 2

ANOTHER PART OF THE GARDEN

ANNE *leads* CHARLOTTE *on. Both women carry parasols.*

ANNE: . . . After I spoke to you, I thought: I will go! I won't! Then I thought: Why not? We'll go to that awful woman's house and I'll say to her: "How dare you try to steal my husband? At your age you should have acquired at least some moral sense." And then — then in the motorcar coming here, I thought: Oh dear, I'll never have the courage and maybe it's all my fault. And oh, I want to go home.

(Bursts into sobs)

CHARLOTTE: Have no fears. Miss Armfeldt has met her match.

ANNE *(Astonished, even through tears)*: She has? Who?

CHARLOTTE: Me. When I told my husband, he instantly became a tiger — his word, of course — and then, as if from heaven, a plan flashed into my mind.

(Pause)

Do you feel up to hearing my plan, dear?

(ANNE gives a little nod)

142

I shall make love to your husband.

ANNE (*Aghast*): You too?

CHARLOTTE: Confident of my own charms, I shall throw myself into your husband's arms. He will succumb. Why not? Carl-Magnus, in a storm of jealousy, will beg my forgiveness and swear eternal fidelity. And as for Miss Desirée Armfeldt, she will be back peddling her dubious commodities elsewhere. At least, that is the plan.

ANNE (*Suddenly forgetful of her tears*): Oh how amusing. How extremely amusing. Poor old Fredrik. And it serves him right, too.

CHARLOTTE: I am not sure I appreciate that remark, dear.
(FREDRIK *appears, walking toward them*)

FREDRIK: Ah, here you are, ladies.

CHARLOTTE (*Sudden devastating smile at* FREDRIK): Oh, Mr. Egerman! If you'll pardon my saying so, that's a simply ravishing cravat.

FREDRIK (*Slightly bewildered*): It is?

CHARLOTTE (*Taking* FREDRIK's *left arm;* ANNE *takes his right arm*): I can't remember when I have seen so seductive a cravat.
(*As* ANNE *suppresses giggles, they all walk off together. As* ANNE, CHARLOTTE, *and* FREDRIK *exit,* MR. LINDQUIST *and* MRS. SEGSTROM *appear*)

MR. LINDQUIST:
The atmosphere's becoming heady,
The ambiance thrilling,

MRS. SEGSTROM:
The spirit unsteady,
The flesh far too willing.

143

MR. LINDQUIST:

    To be perpetually ready
    Is far from fulfilling . . .

MRS. SEGSTROM:

    But wait —
    The sun
    Is dipping.

MR. LINDQUIST:

    Where?
    You're right.
    It's dropping.
    Look — !
    At last!
    It's slipping.

MRS. SEGSTROM:

    Sorry,
    My mistake,
    It's stopping.

                     (*They exit*)

Scene 2A

ANOTHER PART OF THE GARDEN

FREDRIKA *enters.*

FREDRIKA: Oh, I do agree that life at times can seem complicated.

(HENRIK *enters behind her*)

HENRIK: Complicated! If only you knew! Oh, Miss . . . Miss . . .

FREDRIKA: Armfeldt. I am not legitimate.

HENRIK: I see. Oh, Miss Armfeldt, all my life, I've made a fiasco of everything. If you knew how poor an opinion I have of myself! If you knew how many times I wish I had been one of the spermatazoa that never reached the womb.

(*He breaks from her*)

There, there! You see? I've done it again!

FREDRIKA: Mr. Egerman, I have toured with mother, you know. I'm broadminded.

HENRIK: You are? Then in that case, might I make a confession to you?

FREDRIKA: Of course.

145

HENRIK: I hate to burden you on so slight an acquaintance, but bottling it up inside of me is driving me insane.
(*Pause. With great effort*)
Oh, Miss Armfeldt, for the past eleven months, although I am preparing to enter the Ministry, I —
(*He can't get it out*)

FREDRIKA: What, Mr. Egerman?

HENRIK: I have been madly, hopelessly in love with my step-mother. Do you realize how many mortal sins that involves? Oh, damn everything to hell! I beg your pardon.
(*They link arms and walk off.* MR. LINDQUIST, MRS. SEGSTROM, MR. ERLANSON, MRS. ANDERSSEN *and* MRS. NORDSTROM *enter and sing*)

QUINTET:
The light is pink
And the air is still
And the sun is slinking
Behind the hill.
And when finally it sets,
As finally it must,
When finally it lets
The moon and stars adjust,
When finally we greet the dark
And we're breathing Amen —

MRS. ANDERSSEN:
Surprise of surprises,
It instantly rises
Again.

(*The* QUINTET *exits*)

Scene 3

ARMFELDT TERRACE

> *Both dressed for dinner,* FREDRIK *and* CARL-MAGNUS *are discovered;* FREDRIK *downstage,* CARL-MAGNUS *pacing on the porch.* FREDRIK *has a cigar and a small liqueur glass;* CARL-MAGNUS *carries a champagne glass.*

FREDRIK (*Sings, to himself*):
  I should never have
  Gone to the theatre.
  Then I'd never have come
  To the country.
  If I never had come
  To the country,
  Matters might have stayed
  As they were.

CARL-MAGNUS (*Nods*): Sir . . .

FREDRIK (*Nods*): Sir . . .
                      (*To himself again*)
  If she'd only been faded,
  If she'd only been fat,
  If she'd only been jaded
  And bursting with chat,

If she'd only been perfectly awful,
It would have been wonderful.
If . . . if . . .
If she'd been all a-twitter
Or elusively cold,
If she'd only been bitter,
Or better, looked passably old,
If she'd been covered with glitter
Or even been covered with mold,
It would have been wonderful.

But the woman was perfection,
To my deepest dismay.
Well, not quite perfection,
I'm sorry to say.
If the woman were perfection,
She would go away,
And that would be wonderful.

>   (*To* CARL-MAGNUS)

Sir . . .

CARL-MAGNUS: Sir . . .
If she'd only looked flustered
Or admitted the worst,
If she only had blustered
Or simpered or cursed,
If she weren't so awfully perfect,
It would have been wonderful.
If . . .
If . . .
If she'd tried to be clever,
If she'd started to flinch,
If she'd cried or whatever
A woman would do in a pinch,
If I'd been certain she never
Again could be trusted an inch,

It would have been wonderful.

But the woman was perfection,
Not an action denied,
The kind of perfection
I cannot abide.
If the woman were perfection,
She'd have simply lied,
Which would have been wonderful.

FREDRIK:
If she'd only been vicious . . .

CARL-MAGNUS:
If she'd acted abused . . .

FREDRIK:
Or a bit too delicious . . .

CARL-MAGNUS:
Or been even slightly confused . . .

FREDRIK:
If she had only been sulky . . .

CARL-MAGNUS:
Or bristling . . .

FREDRIK:
Or bulky . . .

CARL-MAGNUS:
Or bruised . . .

BOTH:
It would have been wonderful.

CARL-MAGNUS:
If . . .

BOTH:
If . . .

FREDRIK:
If she'd only been willful . . .

CARL-MAGNUS:
If she only had fled . . .

FREDRIK:
Or a little less skillful . . .

CARL-MAGNUS:
Insulted, insisting . . .

FREDRIK:
In bed . . .

CARL-MAGNUS:
If she had only been fearful . . .

FREDRIK:
Or married . . .

CARL-MAGNUS:
Or tearful . . .

FREDRIK:
Or dead . . .

BOTH:
It would have been wonderful.
But the woman was perfection,
And the prospects are grim.
That lovely perfection
That nothing can dim.
Yes, the woman was perfection,
So I'm here with him . . .

CARL-MAGNUS: Sir . . .

FREDRIK: Sir . . .

BOTH:
It would have been wonderful.

(FREDRIKA *enters from the house*)

FREDRIKA: Excuse me, Count Malcolm, but Mother says she
would like a word with you in the green salon.
(CARL-MAGNUS, *glaring triumphantly at* FREDRIK, *strides
into the house.* FREDRIKA *stands and grins shyly at* FREDRIK,
then follows CARL-MAGNUS *into the house.* DESIRÉE *enters*)

DESIRÉE: Fredrik, you wanted a moment alone with me, I
believe. Here it is.

FREDRIK (*Puzzled*): But that child said . . .

DESIRÉE: Oh, that was just Fredrika's little stratagem.

FREDRIK: Fredrika? Your child is called Fredrika?

DESIRÉE: Yes.

FREDRIK: Ah!

DESIRÉE: Really, Fredrik, what vanity. As if you were the only
Fredrik in the world.
(*Brisk*)
Now, what is it you want to tell me?

FREDRIK: As a matter of fact, I thought you should know that
my wife has no inkling of the nightshirt episode. So we
should be discreet.

DESIRÉE: Dear Fredrik, of course. I wouldn't dream of giving
that enchanting child a moment's anxiety.

FREDRIK: Then you do see her charm?

DESIRÉE: How could anyone miss it? How lovely to see you,
Fredrik.

FREDRIK: In spite of Count Malcolm's invasion? You're sure
we're not complicating . . .

CARL-MAGNUS (*Off*): Desirée!

151

FREDRIK: Oh God! Something tells me I should make myself scarce.

CARL-MAGNUS (*Off*): Desirée!

FREDRIK: Later, perhaps?

DESIRÉE: Any time.

FREDRIK: In your room?

DESIRÉE: In my room.
(FREDRIK *looks around for a place to hide. He finds the statue, puts his glass on it, and hides behind it. He douses his cigar in another glass resting on the statue*)

CARL-MAGNUS (*Comes out of the house*): Desirée!

DESIRÉE (*Calling, excessively sweet*): Here, dear!

CARL-MAGNUS: That child said the green salon.

DESIRÉE: She did? How extraordinary.

CARL-MAGNUS: Where's that goddamn lawyer?

DESIRÉE (*Airy*): Mr. Egerman? Oh, somewhere about, no doubt.

CARL-MAGNUS: What's he doing here anyway?

DESIRÉE: He's visiting my mother, of course. He told you. They're the most devoted old friends.

CARL-MAGNUS: That had better be the truth. If I catch him so much as touching you, I'll call him out — with rapiers!
(*Glares*)
Where is your bedroom? Readily accessible, I trust.

DESIRÉE (*Aghast*): But, Carl-Magnus!
(FRID *enters from the house, crosses downstage*)
With your *wife* here . . . !

CARL-MAGNUS: Charlotte is irrelevant. I shall visit your bedroom at the earliest opportunity tonight.

FRID: Madame, Count Malcolm! Dinner is served.
(*As he moves past them to pick up* FREDRIK's *glass, he sees* FREDRIK *behind the statue. Totally unaware of complications*)
Dinner is served, Mr. Egerman.
(FRID *exits up into the house*)

DESIRÉE (*Rising to it*): Ah, there you are, Mr. Egerman!
(FREDRIK *comes out from behind the statue, laughing*)
Gentlemen, shall we proceed?
(*Gives one arm to each as they start up into the house and freeze in place*)

Scene 4

THE DINING ROOM

As the dining room table and guests come on, MRS. NORD-
STROM, MRS. SEGSTROM *and* MRS. ANDERSSEN *sing.*

MRS. NORDSTROM:
Perpetual antici-
  pation is
Good for the soul
But it's bad for the
  heart.
It's very good for
  practicing

Self-control.
It's very good for
Morals,
But bad for morale.
It's very bad.
It can lead to

Going quite mad.
It's very good for

MRS. SEGSTROM:
Perpetual antici-
Pation is good for

The
Soul, but it's bad
For the
Heart.
It's very good for
Practicing self-
Control. It's very
  good for
Morals but bad
For morale. It's

MRS. ANDERSSEN:
Per-
Petual antici-
  pation is good

154

		For
Reserve and	Too unnerving.	The soul, but
		It's
Learning to do	It's very good,	Bad for the
		Heart.
What one should.	Though, to have	It's
It's very good.	Things to contem-	Very good,
		Though,
		To learn to
Perpetual antici-	Plate.	Wait.
pation's		
A delicate art.	Perpetual antici-	
	pation's a	Perpetual
		Anticipation's
		A
Playing a role,	Delicate art.	
		Delicate art.
Aching to start,	Playing a role,	
		Playing a role,
Keeping control	Aching to start,	
		Aching to start,
While falling apart,	Keeping control	
		Keeping control
Perpetual antici-	While falling	
pation is		
	Apart,	While falling
		Apart,
Good for the soul	Perpetual antici-	
	pation is good	Perpetual
		Anticipation
		Is bad for
But it's bad for	But it's bad for	
The heart.	The heart.	The heart.

(The dining room table has moved onstage with MADAME
ARMFELDT *already seated in place, facing the audience in*

solitary splendor. The table is elaborately dressed with fruit and floral pieces and expensive dinnerware. There are also two large candelabra, one at each end of the table. Parallel to the table and upstage of it, the line of servants has come on: BERTRAND, OSA, PETRA, *and* FRID. OSA *and* PETRA *stand with trays as* FRID *and* BERTRAND *light the candelabra.*

Once the table is in place, FREDRIK *and* CARL-MAGNUS *move up to it with* DESIRÉE. FREDRIK *pulls out a chair for* DESIRÉE *and she sits.* FREDRIK *gets* ANNE *and seats her.* CHARLOTTE *enters,* CARL-MAGNUS *seats her on the extreme right end of the table. He then moves to the extreme left, and sits down next to* DESIRÉE. HENRIK *sits between* DESIRÉE *and* ANNE, FREDRIK *between* ANNE *and* CHARLOTTE. *The guests all sit facing upstage.* FRID *and* BERTRAND *pour, and* MADAME ARMFELDT *raises her glass. The others follow her. When the glasses come down, there is a burst of laughter and noise from the guests.* FREDRIKA, *seated at the piano, "accompanies" the scene)*

DESIRÉE: . . . So you won the case after all, Mr. Egerman! How splendid!

FREDRIK: I was rather proud of myself.

DESIRÉE: And I'm sure you were tremendously proud of him too, Mrs. Egerman.

ANNE: I beg your pardon? Oh, I expect so, although I don't seem to remember much about it.
(CHARLOTTE *extends her glass;* BERTRAND *fills it*)

FREDRIK: I try not to bore my wife with my dubious victories in the courtroom.

DESIRÉE: How wise you are. I remember when I was her age, anything less than a new dress, or a ball, or a thrilling piece of gossip bored me to tears.

FREDRIK: That is the charm of youth.

CHARLOTTE: Dearest Miss Armfeldt, do regale us with more fascinating reminiscences from your remote youth.

CARL-MAGNUS: Charlotte, that is an idiotic remark.

FREDRIK: A man's youth may be as remote as a dinosaur, Countess, but with a beautiful woman, youth merely accompanies her through the years.

CHARLOTTE: Oh, Mr. Egerman, that is too enchanting!
(*Leaning over her chair*)
Anne, dear, where on earth did you find this simply adorable husband?

ANNE (*Leans. In on the "plan," of course, giggling*): I'm glad you approve of him.

CHARLOTTE (*To* HENRIK): Your father . . .
(HENRIK *leans*)
is irresistible.
(CARL-MAGNUS *leans*)
I shall monopolize him for the entire weekend.
(DESIRÉE *leans. Then, to* ANNE)
Will you lease him to me, dear?

ANNE (*Giggling*): Freely. He's all yours.
(FREDRIK *looks at* ANNE, *then at* CHARLOTTE, *then leans*)
. . . unless, of course, our hostess has other plans for him.

DESIRÉE (*Smooth, getting out of her seat*): I had thought of seducing him into rolling the croquet lawn tomorrow, but I'm sure he'd find the Countess less exhausting.

CHARLOTTE (*Rising*): I wouldn't guarantee that!
(*Clapping her hand over her mouth*)
Oh, how could those wicked words have passed these lips!

CARL-MAGNUS (*Astonished, rising*): Charlotte!

CHARLOTTE: Oh, Carl-Magnus, dear, don't say you're bristling!

(*To* FREDRIK, *who has also risen. From here the two of them move to the music in a stylized fashion*)

My husband, Mr. Egerman, is a veritable porcupine. At the least provocation he is all spines — or is it quills? Beware. I am leading you down dangerous paths!

CARL-MAGNUS (*Frigid*): I apologize for my wife, sir. She is not herself tonight.

FREDRIK (*Both amused and gracious*): If she is this charming when she is *not* herself, sir, I would be fascinated to meet her when she *is*.

CHARLOTTE: Bravo, bravo! My champion!
(HENRIK *and* ANNE *get up from the table and join the stylized dance*)
May tomorrow find us thigh to thigh pushing the garden roller in tandem.

FREDRIK (*Turning it into a joke*): That would depend on the width of the rollers.
(*To* DESIRÉE)
Miss Armfeldt, as a stranger in this house, may I ask if your roller . . .

CARL-MAGNUS (*Instantly picking this up*): Stranger, sir? How can you call yourself a stranger in *this* house?

FREDRIK (*Momentarily bewildered*): I beg your pardon?

CARL-MAGNUS (*Triumphantly sure he has found* FREDRIK *and* DESIRÉE *out, to* MADAME ARMFELDT): I understand from your daughter, Madame, that Mr. Egerman is an old friend of yours and consequently a frequent visitor to this house.

MADAME ARMFELDT (*Vaguely aware of him, peering through a lorgnette*): Are you addressing me, sir? Whoever you may be.

CARL-MAGNUS: I am, Madame.

158

MADAME ARMFELDT: Then be so kind as to repeat yourself.

DESIRÉE (*Breaking in*): Mother, Count Malcolm —

MADAME ARMFELDT (*Overriding this, ignoring her, to* CARL-MAGNUS): Judging from the level of the conversation so far, young man, you can hardly expect me to have been paying attention.
(CARL-MAGNUS *is taken aback*)

CHARLOTTE: Splendid! The thrust direct! I shall commandeer that remark and wreak havoc with it at all my husband's regimental dinner parties!
(*The guests waltz slowly for a moment. Finally* MADAME ARMFELDT *tings on a glass with her fork for silence*)

MADAME ARMFELDT (*As* FRID *and* BERTRAND *serve*): Ladies and gentlemen, tonight I am serving you a very special dessert wine. It is from the cellars of the King of the Belgians who — during a period of intense intimacy — presented me with all the bottles then in existence. The secret of its unique quality is unknown, but it is said to possess the power to open the eyes of even the blindest among us . . .
(*Raising her glass*)
To Life!
(*The guests all raise their glasses*)

THE GUESTS: To Life!

MADAME ARMFELDT: And to the only other reality — Death!
(*Only* MADAME ARMFELDT *and* CHARLOTTE *drink. A sudden chilly silence descends on the party as if a huge shadow had passed over it. The guests slowly drift back to the table in silence. At length the silence is broken by a little tipsy giggle from* CHARLOTTE)

CHARLOTTE: Oh I *am* enjoying myself! What an unusual sensation!

(*Raises her glass to* DESIRÉE)

Dearest Miss Armfeldt, at this awe-inspiring moment — let me drink to *you* who have made this evening possible. The One and Only Desirée Armfeldt, beloved of hundreds — regardless of course of their matrimonial obligations!

(*Hiccups*)

CARL-MAGNUS: Charlotte, you will go to your room immediately.

(*There is general consternation*)

FREDRIK: Miss Armfeldt, I'm sure the Countess —

ANNE: Oh dear, oh dear, I am beside myself.

HENRIK (*Suddenly jumping up, shouting, smashing his glass on the table*): Stop it! All of you! Stop it!

(*There is instant silence*)

FREDRIK: Henrik!

HENRIK (*Swinging to glare at him*): Are *you* reproving *me?*

FREDRIK: I think, if I were you, I would sit down.

HENRIK: Sit, Henrik. Stand, Henrik. Am I to spend the rest of my life at your command, like a lapdog? Am I to respect a man who can permit such filthy pigs' talk in front of the purest, the most innocent, the most wonderful . . . ? I despise you all!

ANNE (*Giggling nervously*): Oh, Henrik! How comical you look!

DESIRÉE (*Smiling, holding out her glass to him*): Smash this, too. Smash every glass in the house if you feel like it.

HENRIK (*Bewildered and indignant*): And you! You're an artist! You play Ibsen and — and Racine! Don't any of the great truths of the artists come through to you at all? Are you no better than the others?

160

DESIRÉE: Why don't you just laugh at us all, my dear? Wouldn't that be a solution?

HENRIK: How can I laugh, when life makes me want to vomit?

(He runs out of the room)

ANNE: Poor silly Henrik. Someone should go after him.
(She gets up from the table, starts away)

FREDRIK (*Standing, very authoritative*): Anne. Come back.
(Meekly, ANNE obeys, sitting down again at the table. Total silence. FREDRIK sits. Then, after a beat, a hiccup from CHARLOTTE)

DESIRÉE: Dear Countess, may I suggest that you try holding your breath — for a very long time?
(The lights go down on the scene, and the table moves off)

Scene 5

ARMFELDT GARDEN

> HENRIK *runs on and stands near the bench in despair.*
> FREDRIKA, *at the piano, sees him.*

FREDRIKA (*Stops playing*): Mr. Egerman!
> (HENRIK *ignores her*)
>
> Mr. Egerman?
> (HENRIK *looks up*)

HENRIK: I have disgraced myself — acting like a madman, breaking an expensive glass, humiliating myself in front of them all.

FREDRIKA: Poor Mr. Egerman!

HENRIK (*Defending himself in spite of himself*): They laughed at me. Even Anne. She said, "Silly Henrik, how comical you look!" Laughter! How I detest it! Your mother — everyone — says, "Laugh at it all." If all you can do is laugh at the cynicism, the frivolity, the lack of heart — then I'd rather be dead.

ANNE (*Off*): Henrik!

HENRIK: Oh God! There she is!
> (*He runs off*)

162

ANNE (*Off*): Henrik, dear!

FREDRIKA (*Calls after him*): Mr. Egerman! Please don't do anything rash!

(ANNE *runs on*)

Oh, Mrs. Egerman, I'm so terribly worried.

ANNE: You poor dear. What about?

FREDRIKA: About Mr. Egerman — Junior, that is.

ANNE: Silly Henrik! I was just coming out to scold him.

FREDRIKA: I am so afraid he may do himself an injury.

ANNE: How delightful to be talking to someone younger than myself. No doubt he has been denouncing the wickedness of the world — and quoting Martin Luther? Dearest Fredrika, all you were witnessing was the latest crisis in his love affair with God.

FREDRIKA: Not with God, Mrs. Egerman — with you!

ANNE (*Totally surprised*): Me!

FREDRIKA: You may not have noticed, but he is madly, hopelessly in love with you.

ANNE: Is that really the truth?

FREDRIKA: Yes, he told me so himself.

ANNE (*Thrilled, flattered, perhaps more*): The poor dear boy! How ridiculous of him — and yet how charming. Dear friend, if you knew how insecure I constantly feel, how complicated the marriage state seems to be. I adore old Fredrik, of course, but . . .

FREDRIKA (*Interrupting*): But Mrs. Egerman, he ran down towards the lake!

ANNE (*Laughing*): To gaze over the ornamental waters! How touching! Let us go and find him.

(ANNE *takes* FREDRIKA*'s arm and starts walking off with her*)

Such a good looking boy, isn't he? Such long, long lashes . . .
(*They exit giggling, arm-in-arm*)

Scene 5A

ANOTHER PART OF THE GARDEN

> FRID *runs on from behind a screen, followed by a more leisurely* PETRA. *They have a bottle of wine and a small bundle of food with them.*

PETRA: Who needs a haystack? Anything you've got to show, you can show me right here — that is, if you're in the mood.

FRID (*Taking her into his arms*): When am I not in the mood?

PETRA (*Laughing*): I wouldn't know, would I? I'm just passing through.

FRID: I'm in the mood.
(*Kiss*)
I'm in it twenty-four hours a day.
(*Kiss.* FREDRIKA *runs across stage*)

FREDRIKA: Mr. Egerman!

PETRA: Private here, isn't it?
(ANNE *runs across stage*)

ANNE: Henrik! Henrik!

PETRA: What *are* they up to?

FRID: Oh, them! What are they ever up to?

(ANNE *runs back across*)

ANNE: Henrik!

(FREDRIKA *runs back across*)

FREDRIKA: Mr. Egerman!

FRID: You saw them all at dinner, dressed up like waxworks, jabbering away to prove how clever they are. And never knowing what they miss.

(*Kiss*)

ANNE (*Off*): Henrik!

FRID: Catch one of them having the sense to grab the first pretty girl that comes along — and do her on the soft grass, with the summer night just smiling down.

(*Kiss*)

Any complaints yet?

PETRA: Give me time.

FRID: You've a sweet mouth — sweet as honey.

(*The lights dim on them as they lower themselves onto the grass. We now see* HENRIK, *who has been watching them make love. After an anguished moment, he runs straight up into the house, slamming the doors behind him*)

Scene 6

DESIRÉE'S BEDROOM

> DESIRÉE *sits on the bed, her long skirt drawn up over her knees, expertly sewing up a hem.* FREDRIK *enters and clears his throat.*

FREDRIK: Your dragoon and his wife are glowering at each other in the green salon, and all the children appear to have vanished, so when I saw you sneaking up the stairs . . .

DESIRÉE: I ripped my hem on the dining room table in all that furore.

FREDRIK (*Hovering*): Is this all right?

DESIRÉE: Of course. Sit down.
> (*Patting the bed beside her, on which tumbled stockings are strewn*)

FREDRIK: *On* the stockings?

DESIRÉE: I don't see why not.
> (*There is a long pause*)
Well, we're back at the point where we were so rudely interrupted last week, aren't we?

167

FREDRIK: Not quite. If you'll remember, we'd progressed a step further.

DESIRÉE: How true.

FREDRIK: I imagine neither of us is contemplating a repeat performance.

DESIRÉE: Good heavens, with your wife in the house, and my lover and his wife and my daughter . . .

FREDRIK: . . . and my devoted old friend, your mother.
(*They both laugh*)

DESIRÉE (*During it, like a naughty girl*): Isn't my dragoon awful?

FREDRIK (*Laughs*): When you told me he had the brain of a pea, I think you were being generous.
(*They laugh more uproariously*)

DESIRÉE: What in God's name are we laughing about? Your son was right at dinner. We don't fool that boy, not for a moment. The One and Only Desirée Armfeldt, dragging around the country in shoddy tours, carrying on with someone else's dim-witted husband. And the Great Lawyer Egerman, busy renewing his unrenewable youth.

FREDRIK: Bravo! Probably that's an accurate description of us both.

DESIRÉE: Shall I tell you why I really invited you here? When we met again and we made love, I thought: Maybe here it is at last — a chance to turn back, to find some sort of coherent existence after so many years of muddle.
(*Pause*)
Of course, there's your wife. But I thought: Perhaps — just perhaps — you might be in need of rescue, too.

FREDRIK: From renewing my unrenewable youth?

DESIRÉE (*Suddenly tentative*): It was only a thought.

FREDRIK: When my eyes are open and I look at you, I see a woman that I have loved for a long time, who entranced me all over again when I came to her rooms . . . who gives me such genuine pleasure that, in spite of myself, I came here for the sheer delight of being with her again. The woman who could rescue me? Of course.

(Pause)

But when my eyes are not open — which is most of the time — all I see is a girl in a pink dress teasing a canary, running through a sunlit garden to hug me at the gate, as if I'd come home from Timbuktu instead of the Municipal Courthouse three blocks away . . .

DESIRÉE (*Sings*):

Isn't it rich?
Are we a pair?
Me here at last on the ground,
You in mid-air.
Send in the clowns.

Isn't it bliss?
Don't you approve?
One who keeps tearing around,
One who can't move.
Where are the clowns?
Send in the clowns.

Just when I'd stopped
Opening doors,
Finally knowing
The one that I wanted was yours,
Making my entrance again
With my usual flair,
Sure of my lines,
No one is there.

(FREDRIK *rises*)

Don't you love farce?
My fault, I fear.
I thought that you'd want what I want —
Sorry, my dear.
But where are the clowns?
Quick, send in the clowns.
Don't bother, they're here.

FREDRIK: Desirée, I'm sorry. I should never have come. To flirt with rescue when one has no intention of being saved . . . Do try to forgive me.

(*He exits*)

DESIRÉE:

Isn't it rich?
Isn't it queer?
Losing my timing this late
In my career?
And where are the clowns?
There ought to be clowns.
Well, maybe next year . . .

(*The lights iris out on* DESIRÉE)

Scene 7

THE TREES

> *As* DESIRÉE*'s bedroom goes off,* HENRIK *emerges from the house, carrying a rope. He runs downstage with it.* ANNE *and* FREDRIKA *run on; when* HENRIK *hears them, he runs behind a tree to hide.*

ANNE (*As she runs on*): Henrik!
> (*To* FREDRIKA)

Oh, I'm quite puffed! Where can he be?
> (*Noticing* FREDRIKA*'s solemn face*)

Poor child, that face! Don't look so solemn. Where would you go if you were he?

FREDRIKA: Well, the summer pavilion? And then, of course, there's the stables.

ANNE: Then you go to the stables and I'll take the summer pavilion.
> (*Laughing*)

Run!
> (*She starts off*)

Isn't this exciting after that stodgy old dinner!
> (*They run off, and* HENRIK *runs back on. He stops at the tree, stands on the marble bench, and, after circling the*

171

noose around his neck, throws the other end of the rope up to the tree limb. ANNE *can be heard calling "Henrik!"* HENRIK *falls with a loud thud, as* ANNE *enters*)

ANNE: What an extraordinary . . . ! Oh, Henrik — how comical you look!
>   (*Pulling him up by the noose still around his neck*)

Oh, no! You didn't!
>   (*Pause*)

For me?
>   (*She gently removes the noose from his neck*)

Oh, my poor darling Henrik.
>   (*She throws herself into his arms*)

Oh, my poor boy! Oh, those eyes, gazing at me like a lost Saint Bernard . . .
>   (*They start to kiss passionately*)

HENRIK: I love you! I've actually *said* it!

ANNE (*Returning his kisses passionately*): Oh how scatterbrained I was never to have realized. Not Fredrik . . . not poor old Fredrik . . . not Fredrik at all!
>   (*They drop down onto the ground and start to make passionate love. The trees wipe them out, revealing* PETRA *and* FRID. FRID *is asleep*)

PETRA (*Sings*):
  I shall marry the miller's son,
  Pin my hat on a nice piece of property.
  Friday nights, for a bit of fun,
  We'll go dancing.
  Meanwhile . . .

  It's a wink and a wiggle
  And a giggle in the grass
  And I'll trip the light Fandango,
  A pinch and a diddle
  In the middle of what passes by.

It's a very short road
From the pinch and the punch
To the paunch and the pouch and the pension.
It's a very short road
To the ten-thousandth lunch
And the belch and the grouch and the sigh.
In the meanwhile,
There are mouths to be kissed
Before mouths to be fed,
And a lot in between
In the meanwhile.
And a girl ought to celebrate what passes by.

Or I shall marry the businessman,
Five fat babies and lots of security.
Friday nights, if we think we can,
We'll go dancing.
Meanwhile . . .

It's a push and a fumble
And a tumble in the sheets
And I'll foot the Highland Fancy,
A dip in the butter
And a flutter with what meets my eye.
It's a very short fetch
From the push and the whoop
To the squint and the stoop and the mumble.
It's not much of a stretch
To the cribs and the croup
And the bosoms that droop and go dry.
In the meanwhile,
There are mouths to be kissed
Before mouths to be fed,
And there's many a tryst
And there's many a bed
To be sampled and seen

In the meanwhile.
And a girl has to celebrate what passes by.

Or I shall marry the Prince of Wales —
Pearls and servants and dressing for festivals.
Friday nights, with him all in tails,
We'll have dancing.
Meanwhile . . .

It's a rip in the bustle
And a rustle in the hay
And I'll pitch the Quick Fantastic,
With flings of confetti
And my petticoats away up high.
It's a very short way
From the fling that's for fun
To the thigh pressing under the table.
It's very short day
Till you're stuck with just one
Or it has to be done on the sly.
In the meanwhile,
There are mouths to be kissed
Before mouths to be fed,
And there's many a tryst
And there's many a bed.
There's a lot I'll have missed
But I'll not have been dead when I die!
And a person should celebrate everything
Passing by.

And I shall marry the miller's son.
              (*She smiles, as the lights fade on her*)

174

Scene 8

ARMFELDT HOUSE AND GARDEN

> FREDRIKA *is lying on the grass reading.* MADAME ARMFELDT *is seated in a huge wingchair upstage.* DESIRÉE, *on the bed, is writing in her diary.* CARL-MAGNUS *paces on the terrace and then goes into the house.* MRS. SEGSTROM *and* MR. LINDQUIST *are behind trees,* MR. ERLANSON *and* MRS. ANDERSSEN *are behind opposite trees.* CHARLOTTE *sits downstage on a bench. After a beat,* FREDRIK *enters, sees the figure on the bench. Is it* ANNE? *He hurries toward her.*

FREDRIK: Anne? — Oh, forgive me, Countess. I was looking for my wife.

CHARLOTTE (*Looking up, through sobs*): Oh, Mr. Egerman, how can I face you after that exhibition at dinner? Throwing myself at your head!

FREDRIK: On the contrary, I found it most morale-building.
> (*Sits down next to her*)

It's not often these days that a beautiful woman does me that honor.

CHARLOTTE: I didn't.

FREDRIK: I beg your pardon?

175

CHARLOTTE: I didn't do you that honor. It was just a charade. A *failed* charade! In my madness I thought I could make my husband jealous.

FREDRIK: I'm afraid marriage isn't one of the easier relationships, is it?

CHARLOTTE: Mr. Egerman, for a woman it's impossible!

FREDRIK: It's not all that possible for men.

CHARLOTTE: Men! Look at you — a man of an age when a woman is lucky if a drunken alderman pinches her derriere at a village fete! And yet, you have managed to acquire the youngest, prettiest . . . I hate you being happy. I hate *anyone* being happy!

    (HENRIK *and* ANNE *emerge from the house, carrying suitcases. They start stealthily downstage*)

HENRIK: The gig should be ready at the stables.

ANNE (*Giggling*): Oh Henrik, darling, I do hope the horses will be smart. I so detest riding in a gig when the horses are not smart.

    (HENRIK *stops, pulls her to him. They kiss*)

MRS. SEGSTROM (*Turns, looking onstage, sings*):
Think of how I adore you,
Think of how much you love me.
If I were perfect for you,
Wouldn't you tire of me
Soon . . . ?

HENRIK: Let all the birds nest in my hair!

ANNE: Silly Henrik! Quick, or we'll miss the train!

    (*They are now downstage. Unaware of* FREDRIK *and* CHARLOTTE, *they move past them. For a long moment,* FREDRIK *and* CHARLOTTE *sit, while* FREDRIK*'s world tumbles around his ears*)

176

CHARLOTTE: It was, wasn't it?

FREDRIK: It was.

CHARLOTTE: Run after them. Quick. You can catch them at the stables.

FREDRIK (*Even more quiet*): After the horse has gone?
(*Pause*)
How strange that one's life should end sitting on a bench in a garden.

MR. ERLANSON (*Leans, looking onstage, sings*):
She lightens my sadness,
She livens my days,
She bursts with a kind of madness
My well-ordered ways.
My happiest mistake,
The ache of my life . . .
(FREDRIK *and* CHARLOTTE *remain seated as the lights come up on* DESIRÉE*'s bedroom.* CARL-MAGNUS *enters*)

DESIRÉE: Carl-Magnus, go away!

CARL-MAGNUS (*Ignoring her, beginning to unbutton his tunic*):
I'd have been here half an hour ago if I hadn't had to knock a little sense into my wife.

DESIRÉE: Carl-Magnus, do not take off your tunic!

CARL-MAGNUS (*Still ignoring her*): Poor girl. She was somewhat the worse for wine, of course. Trying to make me believe that she was attracted to that asinine lawyer fellow.

DESIRÉE: Carl-Magnus, listen to me! It's over. It was never anything in the first place, but now it's OVER!

CARL-MAGNUS (*Ignoring this, totally self-absorbed*): Of all people — that lawyer! Scrawny as a scarecrow and without a hair on his body, probably.
(*He starts removing his braces*)

177

DESIRÉE (*Shouting*): Don't take off your trousers!

CARL-MAGNUS (*Getting out of his trousers*): Poor girl, she'd slash her wrists before she'd let any other man touch her. And even if, under the influence of wine, she did stray a bit, how ridiculous to imagine I would so much as turn a hair!

(*As he starts to get out of his trouser leg, he stumbles so that he happens to be facing the "window." He stops dead, peering out*)
Good God!

DESIRÉE: What is it?

CARL-MAGNUS (*Peering*): It's her! And him! Sitting on a bench! She's touching him! The scoundrel! The conniving swine! Any man who thinks he can lay a finger on *my* wife!

(*Pulling up his pants and grabbing his tunic as he hobbles out*)

DESIRÉE: Carl-Magnus, what are you doing?

CARL-MAGNUS: My duelling pistols!

(*And he rushes out.* DESIRÉE *runs after him*)

DESIRÉE: Carl-Magnus!

(*The bed rolls off and the lights go down on the bedroom and up on* MADAME ARMFELDT *and* FREDRIKA)

MADAME ARMFELDT: A great deal seems to be going on in this house tonight.

(*Pause*)
Child, will you do me a favor?

FREDRIKA: Of course, Grandmother.

MADAME ARMFELDT: Will you tell me what it's all for? Having outlived my own illusions by centuries, it would be soothing at least to pretend to share some of yours.

178

FREDRIKA (*After thought*): Well, I think it must be worth it.

MADAME ARMFELDT: Why?

FREDRIKA: It's all there is, isn't it? Oh, I know it's often discouraging, and to hope for something too much is childish, because what you want so rarely happens.

MADAME ARMFELDT: Astounding! When I was your age I wanted everything — the moon — jewels, yachts, villas on the Riviera. And I got 'em, too, — for all the good they did me.
(*Music. Her mind starts to wander*)
There was a Croatian Count. He was my first lover. I can see his face now — such eyes, and a mustache like a brigand. He gave me a wooden ring.

FREDRIKA: A wooden ring?

MADAME ARMFELDT: It had been in his family for centuries, it seemed, but I said to myself: a wooden ring? What sort of man would give you a wooden ring, so I tossed him out right there and then. And now — who knows? He might have been the love of my life.
(FREDRIKA *falls asleep, resting her head against* MADAME ARMFELDT*'s knee. In the garden,* FREDRIK *and* CHARLOTTE *pause*)

CHARLOTTE: To think I was actually saying: How I hate you being happy! It's — as if I carry around some terrible curse.
(CARL-MAGNUS *enters from house, runs down steps*)
Oh, Mr. Egerman . . . I'm sorry.
(CHARLOTTE *breaks from* FREDRIK *with a little cry.* FREDRIK, *still dazed, merely turns, gazing vaguely at* CARL-MAGNUS)

CARL-MAGNUS (*Glaring, clicks his heels*): Sir, you will accompany me to the pavilion.

179

(CHARLOTTE *looks at the pistol. Slowly the wonderful truth begins to dawn on her. He really cares! Her face breaks into a radiant smile*)

CHARLOTTE: Carl-Magnus!

CARL-MAGNUS (*Ignoring her*): I think the situation speaks for itself.

CHARLOTTE (*Her ecstatic smile broadening*): Carl-Magnus, dear, you won't be *too* impulsive, will you?

CARL-MAGNUS: Whatever the provocation, I remain a civilized man.
(*Flourishing the pistol*)
The lawyer and I are merely going to play a little Russian Roulette.

CHARLOTTE: Russian Roulette?

CARL-MAGNUS (*To* FREDRIK): Well, sir? Are you ready, sir?

FREDRIK (*Still only half aware*): I beg your pardon. Ready for what??

CHARLOTTE (*Thrilled*): Russian Roulette!

FREDRIK: Oh, Russian Roulette. That's with a pistol, isn't it? And you spin the . . .
(*Indicating*)
Well, why not?
(*Very polite, to* CHARLOTTE)
Excuse me, Madame.
(CARL-MAGNUS *clicks his heels and struts off.* FREDRIK *follows him off slowly*)

MR. LINDQUIST (*Sings*):
A weekend in the country . . .

MR. LINDQUIST *and* MRS. ANDERSSEN:
So inactive

MR. LINDQUIST, MRS. ANDERSSEN *and* MR. ERLANSON:
That one has to lie down.

ALL THE QUINTET:
A weekend in the country
Where . . .
(FRID *and* PETRA *enter, unobserved, and lean against a tree. Gunshot*)
We're twice as upset as in town!
(*The* QUINTET *scatters and runs off, except for* MRS. ANDERSSEN, *who stands behind a tree.* DESIRÉE *runs out of the house and down to* CHARLOTTE)

DESIRÉE: What is it? What's happened?

CHARLOTTE: Oh, dear Miss Armfeldt, my husband and Mr. Egerman are duelling in the pavilion!

DESIRÉE: Are you insane? You let them do it?
(*She starts to run to the pavilion.* CARL-MAGNUS *enters, carrying* FREDRIK *over one shoulder. Quite roughly, he tosses him down on the grass, where* FREDRIK *remains motionless*)

DESIRÉE: You lunatic! You've killed him! Fredrik!

CHARLOTTE: Carl-Magnus!

CARL-MAGNUS: My dear Miss Armfeldt, he merely grazed his ear. I trust his performance in the Law Courts is a trifle more professional.
(*He clears his throat. To* CHARLOTTE)
I am prepared to forgive you, dear. But I feel this house is no longer a suitable place for us.

CHARLOTTE: Oh yes, my darling, I agree!

CARL-MAGNUS: You will pack my things and meet me in the stables. I will have the car ready.

CHARLOTTE: Yes, dear. Oh, Carl-Magnus! You became a tiger for me!

(They kiss)

MRS. ANDERSSEN (Sings):
   Men are stupid, men are vain,
   Love's disgusting, love's insane,
   A humiliating business . . .

MRS. SEGSTROM:
   Oh, how true!
      (CARL-MAGNUS and CHARLOTTE break the kiss. CARL-
      MAGNUS exits. CHARLOTTE runs up to the house)

MRS. ANDERSSEN:
   Aaaah,
      (When CHARLOTTE closes the house doors)
   Well . . .

DESIRÉE: Fredrik? Fredrik!

FREDRIK (Stirs, opens his eyes, looks dazedly around): I don't
   suppose this is my heavenly reward, is it?

DESIRÉE: Hardly, dear, with me here.

FREDRIK (Trying to sit up, failing, remembering): Extraordinary,
   isn't it? To hold a muzzle to one's temple — and yet to
   miss! A shaky hand, perhaps, is an asset after all.

DESIRÉE: Does it hurt?

FREDRIK: It hurts — spiritually. You've heard, I imagine,
   about the evening's other event?

DESIRÉE: No, what?

FREDRIK: Henrik and Anne — ran off together.

DESIRÉE: Fredrik!

FREDRIK: Well, I think I should get up and confront the
   world, don't you?

DESIRÉE (Sings):
   Isn't it rich?

FREDRIK:
Are we a pair?
You here at last on the ground.

DESIRÉE:
You in mid-air.
(*Speaks*)
Knees wobbly?

FREDRIK: No, no, it seems not. In fact, it's hardly possible, but . . .

DESIRÉE (*Sings*):
Was that a farce?

FREDRIK:
My fault, I fear.

DESIRÉE:
Me as a merry-go-round.

FREDRIK:
Me as King Lear.
(*Speaks*)
How unlikely life is! To lose one's son, one's wife, and practically one's life within an hour and yet to feel — relieved. Relieved, and, what's more, considerably less ancient.
(*He jumps up on the bench*)
Aha! Desirée!

DESIRÉE: Poor Fredrik!

FREDRIK: No, no, no. We will banish "poor" from our vocabulary and replace it with "coherent."

DESIRÉE (*Blank*): Coherent?

FREDRIK: Don't you remember your manifesto in the bedroom? A coherent existence after so many years of muddle? You and me, and of course, Fredrika . . .

(*They kiss. The music swells. Sings*)
Make way for the clowns.

DESIRÉE:
Applause for the clowns.

BOTH:
They're finally here.
(*The music continues*)

FREDRIK: How does Malmö appeal to you? It'll be high sunburn season.

DESIRÉE: Why not?

FREDRIK: Why not?

DESIRÉE: Oh God!

FREDRIK: What is it?

DESIRÉE: I've got to do Hedda for a week in Halsingborg.

FREDRIK: Well, what's wrong with Purgatory before Paradise? I shall sit through all eight performances.
(*They go slowly upstage.* FREDRIKA *wakes up*)

FREDRIKA: Don't you think you should go to bed, Grandmother?

MADAME ARMFELDT: No, I shall stay awake all night for fear of missing the first cock-crow of morning. It has come to be my only dependable friend.

FREDRIKA: Grandmother —

MADAME ARMFELDT: What, dear?

FREDRIKA: I've watched and watched, but I haven't noticed the night smiling.

MADAME ARMFELDT: Young eyes are not ideal for watching. They stray too much. It has already smiled. Twice.

FREDRIKA: It has? Twice? For the young — and the fools?

MADAME ARMFELDT: The smile for the fools was particularly broad tonight.

FREDRIKA: So there's only the last to come.

MADAME ARMFELDT: Only the last.

(MADAME ARMFELDT *dies. We become more aware of the underscoring, the same used under the opening waltz.* HENRIK *and* ANNE *suddenly waltz on, and then all of the other couples, at last with their proper partners, waltz through the scene. The trees close in, and* MR. LINDQUIST *appears at the piano. He hits one key of the piano, just as he did at the opening. And the play is over*)

Anne Egerman

Desirée Armfeldt

Countess Celimène de Frances de la Tour de Casa

Desirée Armfeldt

Two of Boris Aronson's set models for
the original Broadway production

Costume designs by Lindsay W. Davis for
the New York City Opera production

ADDITIONAL LYRICS
with Commentary by Stephen Sondheim

"Two Fairy Tales"

Written for the characters of Henrik and Anne Egerman to sing in the first act, "Two Fairy Tales" was cut during the first days of rehearsals as the act was running overlong.

ANNE:
Once upon a time

There lived a princess

Who was exceedingly
  beloved,
Who had a kingdom

Which was perfect,

Which was carpeted with
  jewels.

She was beset on every side

With handsome princes

And lesser nobles

Bearing gifts and begging
  marriage.

She would spurn them,

And they would kill them-
  selves in duels.

HENRIK:
Once upon a time

There lived a knight

Who was devout,

In a kingdom

Which was wretched,

Which was under someone's
  curse.

On every side it was beset

With giant trolls,

And with dragons,

Bringing famine.

He would pray,

And it constantly got worse.
Of course the knight was
  much inspired

195

But the princess soon
  grew tired

By the misery at hand.

Of all the fires she had
  fanned.

And as time went on,

As time went on,

He thought,

She thought, "I must wed
  someone

"I must do something
To alleviate the sorrow
  in the land."

To alleviate the sorrow
  in the land."

Now there were three

There were three

Princes

Dragons
In particular named

In particular named
Virtue,

Falsehood,

Kindness,

Greed,

And Excellence,

And Lust.

But she could not

He could not

Choose

Refuse the call.

At all.

He bade his wife

She bade the three appear.

Farewell, for go he must.
Then to the west

She got her wizard to
  suggest

196

A sort of test.

At her behest

The princely suitors did
their best,

And who'd have guessed?

All three were tested and
they passed.

She was depressed,

To say the least,

But she got dressed

And served a feast
Where she was faced

With princes
Virtue,

Kindness,

And Excellence.

After many years

The king her father,

Who'd been abroad in
search of truth,

The knight set off upon his
quest.

He bore his crest

As if possessed,

Nor did he rest!

He was obsessed.

He found a priest,

He made a fast and was
confessed.

He never ceased,

Until at last he had laid waste

And turned to dust
The dragons

Falsehood,

Greed,

And Lust.

After many years

The noble knight,

Returned to find

The kingdom wretched,

All activity suspended.

To his dismay,
He also found

His daughter mad

With indecision.

She had lapsed into
  a coma,

While her suitors

Had grown restless and
  offended.

And so the king to ease
  her sorrow

Passed a curious decree

That she could marry all
  three suitors.

Did she feel guilty?
No,

Who'd lost an arm,

Returned to find

The kingdom perfect,

All activity resumed.

He also found,
To his dismay,

His wife had died

With the waiting

And his children,

Left alone,

Had been starving and were
  doomed.

So the court upon the
  morrow

Proclaimed a holiday to be,

And the day was named for
  him.
Did he feel guilty?

Oh yes,

And it was wonderful
  to see!
So she lived

Ever after

With Virtue,

Kindness,

And Excellence.

That's a tale

Which was read me by
  my father,

And it was wonderful
  to see!
So he lived —
Not for long —

Ever watchful for

Falsehood,

Greed,

And Lust.

That's a tale
Which was read me by
  my mother,

BOTH:
And there's probably
A moral to be
Pointedly discussed,
But it's always been
My favorite,
And I read it when I'm gloomy,
And though fairy tales are
Foolish, that's a
Fairy tale to trust.

"Silly People"

This number, sung in Scene 5A of Act II, was cut during the show's Boston tryout because it was felt that the character it was written for, Frid, wasn't important enough to spend some four minutes with.

FRID:

    Lie here with me on the grass.
    Let the wind be our words
    As the night smiles down.
    Don't they know, don't they?
    No, they don't, do they?
    Silly people, silly people, silly people.

    Voices glide by, let them pass.
    Let them float in their words
    Till they slowly drown.
    Don't they know, don't they,
    What they want?
    Silly, silly people!
    Patient and polite,
    Crying in their teacups,
    Shying from the night —

    When now it smiles it smiles for lovers.
    When next it smiles it smiles for fools.
    The last it smiles it smiles for them,
    The others, the rememberers,
    The truly silly people.
    Them and us and all . . .

    Lie then with me, closer still.
    You can float in my arms
    Till we gently drown.
    Don't they know, don't they,
    What it means, dying?

Silly people, silly people . . .
Float and flow,
And down we go
To drown.

"Bang!"

To have been sung by Count Carl-Magnus and Desirée in Desirée's digs, this song was cut in rehearsal because it didn't have the transition Hal Prince needed to make the set change that would get the Count from Desiree's digs to his next scene with Charlotte. "Bang!" was replaced by "In Praise of Women," which neatly moved the scene to Charlotte's breakfast nook.

CARL-MAGNUS (*To himself, eyeing Desirée*):
The war commences, the
    enemy awaits
In quivering expectancy.
The poor defenses, the pene-
    trable gates,
How terrible to be a woman.
The time is here,
The game is there.
The smell of fear,
Like musk, pervades the air.
The bugle sounding,
The pistol steady,
The blood is pounding,
Take aim and ready ...
(*Unbuttoning his tunic, one button at a time, with each "Bang!"*)
Bang!
Twenty minutes small talk,
Thirty at the most.
Bang!
Two or three to pour the
    schnapps.
Bang! Bang! Bang!
Half a minute to propose

The necessary toast.
Bang!
The tunic opens,
Bang!
The trousers fall,
Bang!
The foe is helpless,
Back against the wall.
Bang!
An hour and a quarter over
   all,
And bang!

DESIRÉE (*To herself*):
Twenty minutes to arrange
Those bloody awful flowers.

Bang!

Can I get away with more?

Bang! Bang! Bang!

Then I have to brush my
   hair,
And that could take me
   hours.

Bang!

A fit of vapors —

Bang!

No, that's too quaint.

Bang!

A wracking cough,
And then a graceful
   faint . . .

Bang!

A lengthy lecture

Bang!

On self-restraint . . .

Bang! Bang!

QUINTET:
Bang! Bang! Bang! Bang!

The battle rages.

Bang!

Whatever ground I gain
I fortify remorselessly.

Bang! Bang!

The foe engages

Bang!

By shifting the terrain —
How pitiful to be a woman.

Bang!

Attack,

Bang!

Retreat,

Bang!

Lay back,

Bang!

Reform.

Bang! Bang!

Outflank,

Bang!

Deplete,

Bang!

Move up and then restorm.

Bang! Bang! Bang! Bang!

The siege succeeding,

Bang!

The time grows shorter,

Bang!

She lies there pleading,

Bang!

I give no quarter ...
Bang!   Bang!
Foray at the elbow,
Salvo at the knee!
Bang!   Bang!
Fusillades at breast
And thigh!
Bang! Bang! Bang!   Bang! Bang! Bang!
Then when she's exhausted,

Bang!
A fresh sortie!

                Bang!

I taste the conquest,

                Bang!

The taste is sweet.

                Bang! Bang!

She lays her arms down,
Welcoming defeat.

                Bang! Bang!

Both sides, content,

                Bang!

Secure

                Bang!

Positions.

                Bang! Bang! Bang!

All passion spent,

                Bang!

Discuss

                Bang!

Conditions.
How terrible,

                Bang!

How pitiful,

                Bang!

How glorious to be a
  woman.

                DESIRÉE:
                He is a peacock,
                I keep forgetting . . .

The quarry senses
A momentary pang.

                It's all so foolish —
                Why am I sweating?

The war commences.
Bang!

"My Husband the Pig"

"My Husband the Pig" was written to be sung in Act I, Scene 5 by Charlotte, angrily trying to enjoy her breakfast after Carl-Magnus has ordered her to pay a visit to the Egerman household. It was replaced by the second half of "In Praise of Women."

CHARLOTTE:

Fop.
Lout.
What am I, a prop
To order about?
Adulterous lowlife!
He seems to assume I have no life
Of my own.
Well, he isn't alone!

I lie on the shelf at my station
To bolster his self-adulation.
I have no objection
To passing inspection,
But who can contend with an endless erection
That falls on its knees when it sees its reflection?

My husband, the pig,
The swaggering bore
I'll do anyting for,
What a pig!
The air of disdain is appalling,
The level of decency nil.
If he thinks that I'll always come crawling,
Ha! I will.

My husband, the pig.
I worship the ground
That he kicks me around
On, the pig.

A stunted affront to humanity,
A vat of gelatinous vanity,
The stamp of my rampant insanity:
My husband the —

Ugh!
There's a clot in the cream
And a fly in the jam
And I think that I'm going to scream. . . . .
Yes, I am!
But would anyone here give a damn?
No.

Ah, well.
Every day a little death
In the parlor, in the bed,
In the curtains, in the silver,
In the buttons, in the bread.
Every day a little sting
In the heart and in the head.
Every move and every breath,
And you hardly feel a thing,
Brings a perfect little death.

Every day a little death,
On the lips and in the eyes
In the murmurs, in the pauses,
In the gestures, in the sighs.
Every day a little dies
In the looks and in the lies,
And you hardly feel a thing . . .

Ugh!
There's a leaf in the cup
And a crack in the pot
And I think I'm about to throw up.
But I'm not,

'Cause I have to go out, and for what?

A pat on the hand and I'm suet.
I don't understand why I do it.
While I'm in abstention
In every dimension,
His horse and his whores and his wars get attention
And I decompose like a rose with a pension!

My husband, the pig.
I loathe and deplore
Every bone I adore,
He's a pig!
He throws me a crumb to be cruel
And then expects humble delight.
Does he think a duet is a duel?
Ha! He's right!

My husband, the pig!
My swain is a swine
Or, to further refine
It, a pig!
It's ghastly and vastly ironical,
A cynical, clinical chronicle:
"The woman who married a monocle."
My husband, the pig!
Ugh!

"Night Waltz" ("Love Takes Time")

As the opening for the motion picture, these lyrics were written for "Night Waltz."

DESIRÉE, CHARLOTTE, ANNE, PETRA, MADAME ARMFELDT,
FREDERICKA, ERICH, FREDERICK:
Love takes time,
Entirely too much but sublime.
Frightening, love is.
Full of quicksand,
Enlightening, love is,
Full of tricks and
It does take time,
Which really is rather a crime.

Curious, love is,
Self-tormenting,
Embarrassing, love is,
Unrelenting,
A labyrinth, love is.
Just resenting
The time love takes
Compounds the confusion it makes.
One muddles the facts with the fakes.
And love is a lecture
On how to correct your
Mistakes.
                    (*Individual voices*)
What shall I wear?
Where is my parasol?
Do I compare?
                    (*Overlapping*)
Have I missed it?
Will I ever?

209

    Did he notice?
    What will they say?
    Should I care?
    How does one start it up again?
    Why can't we stay just the way — ?
    Will I ever?
    Was I ever?
    Can I ever?

MADAME ARMFELDT: I have no questions ...

OTHERS:
    Love comes first.
    It matters the most at its worst.
    You always feel underrehearsed.
    One sets the conditions,
    Then finds the positions
    Reversed.
    The time love takes
    Awakens the heart that it breaks.
    Consider the new friends it makes.
    Yes, love is a lecture
    On how to correct your
    Mistakes.
                    (*Overlapping*)
    What shall I wear?
    Where is my parasol?
    Do I compare?
    Would she dare?
    Have I missed it?
    Will I ever?

MADAME ARMFELDT: I have no time ...

OTHERS (*All overlapping, gradually fading*):
    Why did she smile? Will she remember?
    Why are we laughing? What will he want?

Are you ever? Do you ever?
When will I learn?
Am I too late?
Why did I say that? Is there time? Am I too late?
Have I the right? What are the chances?
Where is my parasol? . . .

"The Glamorous Life"

In the stage version of Night Music, *"The Glamorous Life" is a song about Desirée's life as an actress on the road, with three different points of view — Fredrika's, Desirée's and Madame Armfeldt's — but it was felt that this would be too convoluted and confusing for the film version, and the song was rewritten preserving only the verse of the number (with new lyrics) and employing only one point of view, Fredericka's.*

FREDERICKA:

Ordinary mothers lead ordinary lives,
Mop the floors and chop the parsley,
Mend the clothes and tend the children.
Ordinary mothers, like ordinary wives,
Make the beds and bake the pies
And wither on the vine —
Not mine.

Dying by inches
Every night,
What a glamorous life!
Pulled on by winches
To recite —
What a glamorous life!

Ordinary mothers never get the flowers
And ordinary mothers never know the joys,
But ordinary mothers couldn't cough for hours,
Maintaining their poise.

Sandwiches only,
But she eats
What she wants when she wants.
Sometimes it's lonely,

But she meets
Many handsome gallants.

Ordinary mothers don't live out of cases
But ordinary mothers don't go different places,
Which ordinary mothers can't do,
Being mothers all day.
Mine's away in a play
And she's realer than they ...

What if her brooch is only glass
And her costumes unravel?
What if her coach is second class?
She at least gets to travel.

And some time this summer,
Meaning soon,
She'll be travelling to me!
Some time this summer —
Maybe June —
I'm the new place she'll see!

Ordinary daughters may think life is better
With ordinary mothers near them when they choose,
But ordinary daughters seldom get a letter
Enclosing reviews!

Gay and resilient,
With applause —
What a glamorous life!
Speeches are brilliant —
When they're Shaw's —
What a glamorous life!

Ordinary mothers needn't meet committees,

But ordinary mothers don't get keys to cities.
No, ordinary mothers merely see their children all year —
Which is lovely, I hear,
But it does interfere
With the glamorous ...

I am the princess, guarded by dragons
Snorting and grumbling and rumbling in wagons.
She's in her kingdom, wearing disguises,
Living a life that is full of surprises,

And some time this summer
She'll come galloping over the green!
Some time this summer,
To my rescue, my mother the queen!

Ordinary mothers thrive on being private,
But ordinary mothers somehow can survive it,
And ordinary mothers never know they're just standing
    still,
With the kettles to fill,
While they're missing the thrill
Of the glamorous life!

"Send in the Clowns"

For Barbra Streisand's recording of this song on her Broadway
Album, *the lyrics were slightly revised, and a new lyric written for
a second release.*

Isn't it rich?
Are we a pair?
Me here at last on the ground,
You in mid-air.
Send in the clowns.

Isn't it bliss?
Don't you approve?
One who keeps tearing around,
One who can't move.
Where are the clowns?
Send in the clowns.

Just when I'd stopped
Opening doors,
Finally knowing
The one that I wanted was yours,
Making my entrance again
With my usual flair,
Sure of my lines,
No one is there.

Don't you love farce?
My fault, I fear.
I thought that you'd want what I want —
Sorry, my dear.
But where are the clowns?
There ought to be clowns.
Quick, send in the clowns.

What a surprise!

Who could foresee
I'd come to feel about you
What you felt about me?
Why only now when I see
That you've drifted away?
What a surprise . . .
What a cliché . . .

Isn't it rich?
Isn't it queer?
Losing my timing this late
In my career?
And where are the clowns?
Quick, send in the clowns!
Don't bother, they're here.

MAJOR PRODUCTIONS

A Little Night Music was first presented by Harold Prince, in association with Ruth Mitchell, at the Sam S. Shubert Theatre, New York City, on February 25, 1973, with the following cast:

(in order of appearance)

MR. LINDQUIST	Benjamin Rayson
MRS. NORDSTROM	Teri Ralston
MRS. ANDERSSEN	Barbara Lang
MR. ERLANSON	Gene Varrone
MRS. SEGSTROM	Beth Fowler
FREDRIKA ARMFELDT	Judy Kahan
MADAME ARMFELDT	Hermione Gingold
FRID, *her butler*	George Lee Andrews
HENRIK EGERMAN	Mark Lambert
ANNE EGERMAN	Victoria Mallory
FREDRIK EGERMAN	Len Cariou
PETRA	D. Jamin-Bartlett
DESIRÉE ARMFELDT	Glynis Johns
MALLA, *her maid*	Despo
BERTRAND, *a page*	Will Sharpe Marshall
COUNT CARL-MAGNUS MALCOLM	Laurence Guittard
COUNTESS CHARLOTTE MALCOLM	Patricia Elliott
OSA	Sherry Mathis

Production Directed by Harold Prince
Choreography by Patricia Birch
Scenic Production Designed by Boris Aronson
Costumes Designed by Florence Klotz
Lighting Designed by Tharon Musser
Orchestrations by Jonathan Tunick
Musical Direction by Harold Hastings

219

The following songs were cut prior to the New York opening: "*Silly People*," "*Two Fairy Tales*," "*My Husband the Pig*," and "*Bang!*"

A Little Night Music gave its first performance at the Colonial Theatre in Boston, opening on January 23, 1973 and closing on February 10th after 23 performances. Previews began in New York City on February 14, 1973, and the show opened on February 25th and closed on August 3, 1974 after 601 performances and 12 previews.

AWARDS

New York Drama Critics Circle Award — Best Musical

Tony Awards: Best Musical, Best Book of a Musical (Hugh Wheeler), Best Music and Lyrics (Stephen Sondheim), Best Actress in a Musical (Glynis Johns), Best Supporting Actress in a Musical (Patricia Elliott), Best Costume Design (Florence Klotz). Also received Tony nominations for Best Direction of a Musical (Harold Prince), Best Actor in a Musical (Len Cariou), Best Supporting Actor in a Musical (Laurence Guittard), Best Supporting Actress in a Musical (Hermione Gingold), Best Scenic Design (Boris Aronson) and Best Lighting Design (Tharon Musser).

A Little Night Music was first presented in London by Ruth Mitchell, Frank Milton, Eddie Kulukundis and Richard Pilbow, in association with Bernard Delfont, at the Adelphi Theatre on April 15, 1975 for 406 performances, with the following cast:

(in order of appearance)

MR. LINDQUIST	John J. Moore
MRS. NORDSTROM	Chris Melville
MRS. ANDERSSEN	Liz Robertson
MR. ERLANSON	David Bexon
MRS. SEGSTROM	Jacquey Chappell
FREDRIKA ARMFELDT	Christine McKenna
MADAME ARMFELDT	Hermione Gingold
FRID, *her butler*	Michael Harbour
HENRIK EGERMAN	Terry Mitchell
ANNE EGERMAN	Veronica Page
FREDRIK EGERMAN	Joss Ackland
PETRA	Diane Langton
DESIRÉE ARMFELDT	Jean Simmons
BERTRAND, *a page*	Christopher Beeching
COUNT CARL-MAGNUS MALCOLM	David Kernan
COUNTESS CHARLOTTE MALCOLM	Maria Aitken
OSA	Penelope Potter

Production Directed by Harold Prince
Choreography by Patricia Birch
Production Supervised by George Martin
Scenic Production Designed by Boris Aronson
Costumes Designed by Florence Klotz
Lighting Designed by Tharon Musser
Orchestrations by Jonathan Tunick
Musical Direction by Ray Cook
Sound by David Collison

AWARD: London Standard Drama Award for Best Musical

A Little Night Music was revived in London by H. M. Tennent Ltd., by arrangement with the Chichester Festival Theatre, John Gale, Executive Producer, at the Piccadilly Theatre, October 6, 1989 – February 17, 1990 for 144 performances, with the following cast:

MADAME ARMFELDT	Lila Kedrova
DESIRÉE ARMFELDT, *her daughter*	Dorothy Tutin
FREDRIKA ARMFELDT, *her granddaughter*	Debra Beaumont
FRID, *her manservant*	David Hitchen
FREDRIK EGERMAN, *a lawyer*	Peter McEnery
HENRIK EGERMAN, *his son*	Alexander Hanson
ANNE EGERMAN, *his second wife*	Deborah Poplett
PETRA, *their maid*	Sara Weymouth
COUNT CARL-MAGNUS MALCOLM	Eric Flynn
COUNTESS CHARLOTTE MALCOLM, *his wife*	Susan Hampshire
MALLA	Mandi Martin
OSA	Susan Paule

The Liebeslieder Singers

MRS. NORDSTROM	Dinah Harris
MRS. ANDERSSEN	Hilary Western
MRS. SEGSTROM	Susan Flannery
MR. ERLANSON	Michael Bulman
MR. LINDQUIST	Martin Nelson

Directed by Ian Judge
Designed by Mark Thompson
Choreography by Anthony Van Laast
Lighting by Nick Chelton
Sound by Matthew Gale
Music Supervised by John Owen Edwards
Musical Director, Roger Ward

A Little Night Music was presented by the New York City Opera (Christopher Keene, General Director) at the New York State Theatre, New York City, August 3, 1990, with the following cast:

MR. LINDQUIST	Ron Baker
MRS. NORDSTROM	Lisa Saffer
MRS. ANDERSSEN	Barbara Shirvis
MR. ERLANSON	Michael Rees Davis
MRS. SEGSTROM	Susanne Marsee
FREDRIKA ARMFELDT	Danielle Ferland
MADAME ARMFELDT	Regina Resnik
FRID, *her butler*	David Comstock
HENRIK EGERMAN	Kevin Anderson
ANNE EGERMAN	Beverly Lambert
FREDRIK EGERMAN	George Lee Andrews
PETRA	Susan Terry
DESIRÉE ARMFELDT	Sally Ann Howes
MALLA, *her maid*	Raven Wilkinson
BERTRAND, *a page*	Michael Rees Davis
COUNT CARL-MAGNUS MALCOLM	Michael Maguire
COUNTESS CHARLOTTE MALCOLM	Maureen Moore
OSA	Judith Jarosz

SERVANTS: Michael Cornell, Ernest Foederer, Kent A. Heacock, Ronald Kelley, Brian Michaels, Brian Quirk, Christopher Shepherd, John Henry Thomas.

Conducted by Paul Gemignani
Directed by Scott Ellis
Orchestrations by Jonathan Tunick
Scenery Designed by Michael Anania
Costumes Designed by Lindsay W. Davis
Lighting Designed by Dawn Chiang
Choreography by Susan Stroman
Sound Designed by Abe Jacob

The motion picture of *A Little Night Music* was produced by New World/Sascha-Wien Films, in association with Elliott Kastner, and released in March of 1978, with the following cast:

DESIRÉE ARMFELDT	Elizabeth Taylor
CHARLOTTE MITTELHEIM	Diana Rigg
FREDERICK EGERMAN	Len Cariou
ANNE EGERMAN	Lesley-Anne Down
MME. ARMFELDT	Hermione Gingold
CARL-MAGNUS MITTELHEIM	Laurence Guittard
ERICH EGERMAN	Christopher Guard
FREDERICKA ARMFELDT	Chloe Franks
KURT	Heins Marecek
PETRA	Lesley Dunlop
CONDUCTOR	Jonathan Tunick
FRANZ	Herbert Tscheppe
BAND CONDUCTOR	Rudolph Schrympf
THE MAYOR	Franz Schussler
THE MAYORESS	Johanna Schussler
BOX OFFICE LADY IN THEATRE	Jean Sincere
FIRST LADY	Dagmar Koller
SECOND LADY	Ruth Brinkman
CONCIERGE	Anna Veigl
UNIFORMED SARGEANT	Stefan Paryla
FIRST WHORE	Eva Dvorska
SECOND WHORE	Lisa De Cohen
MAJOR DOMO	Kurt Martynow
COOK	Gerty Barek
FOOTMAN	James De Groat

(Note: For the film the locale was changed from Sweden to Vienna, and some of the character names were Germanized.)

Directed by Harold Prince
Screenplay by Hugh Wheeler
Edited by John Jympson
Photographed by Arthur Ibbetson, B.S.C.
Costumes Designed by Florence Klotz
Choreography by Patricia Birch
Music Scored and Supervised by Jonathan Tunick
Musical Direction by Paul Gemignani
Executive Producer, Heinz Lazek
Presented by Roger Corman — A New World Picture

MUSICAL NUMBERS

"Overture"/"Night Waltz" (*"Love Takes Time"*)	Company
"The Glamorous Life"	Chloe Franks
"Now"/"Soon"/"Later"	Len Cariou, Lesley-Anne Down, Christopher Guard
"You Must Meet My Wife"	Len Cariou, Elizabeth Taylor
"Every Day a Little Death"	Diana Rigg
Night Waltz	Instrumental
"A Weekend in the Country"	Company
"Send in the Clowns"	Elizabeth Taylor
"It Would Have Been Wonderful"	Len Cariou, Laurence Guittard
Finale: "Send in the Clowns"/"Night Waltz"	Len Cariou, Elizabeth Taylor, Company

The motion picture is available on video cassette: Embassy Home Entertainment 00103.

SELECTED DISCOGRAPHY

* Original Broadway Cast Recording (1973)

Columbia Records
LP KS (S)/SQ (Q)-32265
Cassette ST 32265
CD CK 32265
(Also included in Time-Life Records "American Musicals" series:
Stephen Sondheim. LP STL–AM12, Cassette 4TL–AM12)
(Although recorded for the original cast album, *"Night Waltz II"*
was not included on the final original cast recording)

+ Original London Cast Recording (1975)

RCA Records
LP LRL1-5090 (S)
Cassette CRK1-5090; reissue 5090-4-RG
CD RCD1-5090; reissue 5090-2-RG

Motion Picture Soundtrack Recording (1978)

Columbia Records
LP JS 35333 (S)
Cassette JST 35333

A Little Night Music (studio cast recording, 1990)

That's Entertainment Records (England)
Cassette ZCTER 1179
CD CDTER 1179
(Includes *"Night Waltz II"*)

Sondheim: A Musical Tribute (1973)

Warner Bros. Records
LP 2WS 2705 (S); 2 record set
RCA Records (1990 reissue)
Cassette 60515-4
CD 60515-2
Includes: *"Silly People"*—George Lee Andrews; *"Two Fairy
Tales"*—Mark Lambert, Victoria Mallory

---

* Winner of the Grammy Award for Best Original Cast Show Album
+ Nominated for the Grammy Award for Best Original Cast Show Album
Note: *"Send in the Clowns"* won the 1975 Grammy for Song of the Year,
with the award going to Mr. Sondheim as the composer/lyricist.

Side by Side by Sondheim/Millicent Martin, Julia McKenzie and David Kernan (1976)

    RCA Records

        LP CBL2–1851 (S); 2 record set

        Cassette CBK2–1851; reissue 1851-4-RG

        CD 1851-2-RG; 2 disc set

      Includes: *"You Must Meet My Wife"*—David Kernan, Millicent Martin; *"Send in the Clowns"*—Millicent Martin

Songs of Sondheim (original Irish cast recording of *Side by Side by Sondheim,* 1977)

    RAM Records

        LP RMLP 1026

      Includes: *"Send in the Clowns"*—Gemma Craven

Side by Side by Sondheim (original Australian cast recording, 1977)

    RCA Red Seal (Australia)

        LP VRL2–0156; 2 record set

        Cassette VRK2–0156; 2 tape set

      Includes: *"You Must Meet My Wife"*—Bartholomew John, Jill Perryman; *"Send in the Clowns"*—Jill Perryman

A Different Side of Sondheim/Richard Rodney Bennett (1979)

    DRG Records

        LP SL 5182

        Cassette SLC–5182

      Includes: *"You Must Meet My Wife," "Night Waltz I"*

Marry Me a Little/Craig Lucas and Suzanne Henry (1981)

    RCA Records

        LP ABL1–4159 (S)

        Cassette ABK1–4159; reissue 7142-4-RG

        CD 7142-2-RG

      Includes: *"Two Fairy Tales"*—Craig Lucas, Suzanne Henry; *"Bang!"*—Craig Lucas, Suzanne Henry; *"Silly People"*—Craig Lucas

Evelyn Lear Sings Sondheim and Bernstein (1981)
Mercury Records Golden Imports
LP MR 75136
Cassette MRI 75136
Includes: *"Send in the Clowns"*

A Stephen Sondheim Collection/Jackie Cain and Roy Kral (1982)
Finesse Records
LP FW 38324 (S)
Cassette FWT 38324
DRG Records (1990 reissue)
Cassette DSC 25102
CD DSCD 25102
Includes: *"Send in the Clowns"*—Jackie Cain

A Stephen Sondheim Evening (1983)
RCA Records
LP CBL2–4745 (S); 2 record set
Cassette CBK2–4745; 2 tape set
Includes: *"Send in the Clowns"*—Angela Lansbury; *"The Miller's Son"*
—Liz Callaway

A Little Sondheim Music/Los Angeles Vocal Arts Ensemble (1984)
Angel Records
LP EMI DS-37347 (S)
Cassette EMI 4DS-37347
Includes: *"Overture"*—Michael Gallup, Darlene Romano, Delcina
Stevenson, Jeffrey Araluce, Rickie Weiner-Gole; *"Night
Waltz I"*/*"Night Waltz II"*—Janet Smith, Darlene Romano,
Paul Johnson, Rickie Weiner-Gole, Michael Gallup; *"In
Praise of Women"*—Michael Gallup; *"A Weekend in the
Country"*—Janet Smith, Michael Gallup, Ensemble; *"Send in
the Clowns"* —Rickie Weiner-Gole, Dale Morich

The Broadway Album/Barbra Streisand (1985)
Columbia Records
LP OC 40092
Cassette OCT 40092
CD CK 40092
Includes: *"Send in the Clowns"* (with Sondheim's revised lyric)

A Collector's Sondheim (1985)
RCA Records
LP CRL4–5359 (S); 4 record set
Cassette CRK4–5359; 4 tape set
CD RCD3–5480; 3 disc set
Includes: *"Overture"*/*"Night Waltz I"*—Orchestra/John J. Moore, Chris
Melville, Liz Robertson, David Bexon, Jacquey Chappell;
"The Glamorous Life"—Christine McKenna, Jean Simmons,
John J. Moore, Chris Melville, Liz Robertson, David Bexon,
Jacquey Chappell, Hermione Gingold; *"In Praise of
Women"*—David Kernan; *"A Weekend in the Country"*—Diane
Langton, Veronica Page, Joss Ackland, Maria Aitken, David
Kernan, Terry Mitchell; *"Liaisons"*—Hermione Gingold;
"The Miller's Son"—Diane Langton (all six tracks from origi-
nal London cast recording); *"Two Fairy Tales"*—Craig Lucas,
Suzanne Henry; *"Silly People"*—Craig Lucas (not included
on CD release); *"Bang!"*—Craig Lucas, Suzanne Henry (all
three tracks from original cast recording of *Marry Me a
Little*); *"The Glamorous Life"* (The Letter Song)—Elaine
Tomkinson (track from the motion picture soundtrack);
"Night Waltz II"—Teri Ralston, Gene Varrone, Benjamin
Rayson, Beth Fowler, Barbara Lang (out-take from original
Broadway cast recording); *"Send in the Clowns"*—Angela
Lansbury (track from *A Stephen Sondheim Evening*)

Sondheim (1985)
Book-of-the-Month Records
LP 81–7515 (S); 3 record set
Cassette 91–7516; 2 tape set
CD 11–7517; 2 disc set
Includes: *"Liaisons"*—Chamber Ensemble; *"Send in the Clowns"*—Joyce
Castle; *"You Must Meet My Wife"*—Chamber Ensemble; *"The
Glamorous Life"* (The Letter Song)—Betsy Joslyn (the
motion picture version)

Old Friends/Geraldine Turner Sings the Songs of Stephen Sondheim (1986)
Larrikin Records (Australia)
  LP LRF-169
  Cassette TC-LRF-169
Includes: *"The Miller's Son"*
(This album was reissued by Silva Screen Records [London] under the title *The Stephen Sondheim Songbook*: LP Song 001, Cassette Song C001, CD Song CD001)

Cleo Sings Sondheim/Cleo Laine (1988)
RCA Records
  LP 7702–1–RC
  Cassette 7702–4–RC
  CD 7702–2–RC
Includes: *"Liaisons," "Send in the Clowns," "The Miller's Son"*

Julie Wilson Sings the Stephen Sondheim Songbook (1988)
DRG Records
  LP SL 5206
  Cassette SLC 5206
  CD CDSL 5206
Includes: *"Send in the Clowns"*

The Other Side of Sondheim/Jane Harvey (1988)
Atlantic Records
  LP 81833-1
  Cassette 81833-4
  CD 81833-2
Includes: *"Send in the Clowns"*

Symphonic Sondheim/Don Sebesky Conducts The London Symphony Orchestra (1990)
WEA Records (London)
  LP 9031-72 119-1
  Cassette 9031-72 119-4
  CD 9031-72 119-2
Includes: *"Send in the Clowns"*

Stephen Sondheim wrote the music and lyrics for *A Funny Thing Happened on the Way to the Forum* (1962), *Anyone Can Whistle* (1964), *Company* (1970), *Follies* (1971), *A Little Night Music* (1973), *The Frogs* (1974), *Pacific Overtures* (1976), *Sweeney Todd, the Demon Barber of Fleet Street* (1979), *Merrily We Roll Along* (1981), *Sunday in the Park with George* (1984), *Into the Woods* (1986) and *Assassins* (1990), the lyrics for *West Side Story* (1957, music by Leonard Bernstein), *Gypsy* (1959, music by Jule Styne) and *Do I Hear a Waltz?* (1965, music by Richard Rodgers), and additional lyrics for a new production of *Candide* (1973, music by Leonard Bernstein). He provided incidental music for the plays *The Girls of Summer* (1956), *Invitation to a March* (1961), *Twigs* (1971) and *The Enclave* (1973). He wrote the music and lyrics for the television production *Evening Primrose* (1966), composed the film scores for *Stavisky* (1974) and *Reds* (1981), wrote songs for the motion pictures *The Seven Percent Solution* (1976) and *Dick Tracy* (1990) and co-authored the film *The Last of Sheila* (1973). He won Tony Awards for his scores for *Company, Follies, A Little Night Music, Sweeney Todd* and *Into the Woods*, and all of these musicals won the New York Drama Critics Circle Award for Best Musical, as did *Pacific Overtures* and *Sunday in the Park with George*, the latter also receiving the Pulitzer Prize in 1985. Mr. Sondheim is on the Council of the Dramatists Guild, having served as its president from 1973 to 1981, was elected to the American Academy and Institute of Arts and Letters in 1983, received the London Evening Standard Award in 1989 for his contribution to the musical theater, and in 1989 was named the first Visiting Professor of Contemporary Theatre at Oxford University.

Hugh Wheeler was a novelist, playwright and screen writer. He wrote more than thirty mystery novels under the pseudonyms Q. Patrick and Patrick Quentin, and four of his novels were transformed into films: *Black Widow, Man in the Net, The Green-Eyed Monster* and *The Man with Two Wives*. For films he wrote the screenplays for *Travels with My Aunt, Something for Everyone, A Little Night Music* and *Nijinsky*. His plays include *Big Fish, Little Fish* (1961), *Look: We've Come Through* (1961) and *We Have Always Lived in the Castle* (1966, adapted from the Shirley Jackson novel), he co-authored with Joseph Stein the book for a new production of the

1919 musical *Irene* (1973), wrote the books for *A Little Night Music* (1973), a new production of *Candide* (1973), *Sweeney Todd, the Demon Barber of Fleet Street* (1979, based on a version of the play by Christopher Bond), and *Meet Me in St. Louis* (adapted from the 1949 M-G-M musical), contributed additional material for the musical *Pacific Overtures* (1976), and wrote a new adaptation of the Kurt Weill opera *Silverlake*, which was directed by Hal Prince at the New York Opera. He received Tony and Drama Desk Awards for *A Little Night Music, Candide* and *Sweeney Todd*. Prior to his death in 1987 Mr. Wheeler was working on two new musicals, *Bodo* and *Fu Manchu*, and a new adaptation of *The Merry Widow*.

Jonathan Tunick, long regarded as Broadway's pre-eminent orchestrator, has contributed to the success of such landmark productions as *Sweeney Todd, Follies, A Little Night Music, Company, A Chorus Line* and *Into the Woods*. He has also composed and conducted over thirty scores for motion pictures and television, including PBS's American Masters series and his Emmy-nominated scores for *Concealed Enemies* on PBS and NBC's *Tattinger's*. He is Music Director of the Opera Ensemble of New York, where he specializes in conducting classic light opera and musicals. He was the conductor of the CBS recording of Rodgers and Hammerstein's *South Pacific* with Kiri Te Kanawa and the London Symphony Orchestra. He has long been associated with Judy Collins as arranger-conductor, and is soon to perform in the same capacity on a new EMI recording with Placido Domingo and Itzhak Perlman. He has received the Emmy and Drama Desk Awards, and for his work on the film version of *A Little Night Music*, the Academy Award. Last season he was awarded a Grammy as arranger-conductor of the RCA album *Cleo Sings Sondheim*. The New Grove Dictionary of American Music describes him as "A skillful technician, whose sympathetic understanding of orchestral instruments is often employed to heighten the dramatic effect of a work." Martin Gottfried, in *The Broadway Musical*, refers to him as ". . . the finest orchestrator in our theater's history."